# Tragedy On Greasy Ridge

true stories from Appalachian Ohio

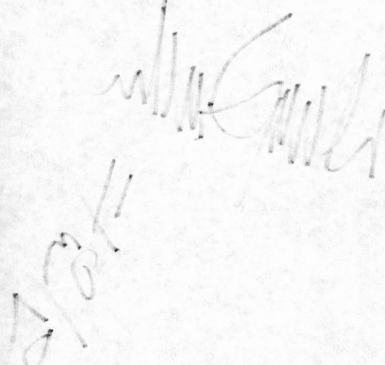

# Tragedy On Greasy Ridge

true stories from Appalachian Ohio

by
Danny Fulks

Jesse Stuart Foundation
Ashland, Kentucky
2003

*For: Michael, Emily, Andrew, Gary, Daniel,*
*Candy Sue, and Cathy Lynn*

Library of Congress Cataloging-in-Publication Data

Fulks, Danny, 1933-
    Tragedy on Greasy Ridge: true stories from Appalachian Ohio / by Danny Fulks.—1st ed.
    p. cm.
    ISBN 1-931672-15-6
    1. Ohio—History, Local—Anecdotes. 2. Appalachian Region—History, Local—Anecdotes. 3. Ohio—Biography—Anecdotes. 4. Appalachian Region—Biography—Anecdotes. 5. Ohio—Social life and customs—Anecdotes. 6. Appalachian Region—Social life and customs—Anecdotes. 7. Mountain life—Ohio—Anecdotes. 8. Mountain life—Appalachian Region—Anecdotes. 9. Fulks, Danny, 1933—Anecdotes. I. Title.

F491.6.F85 2003
977.1'9—dc21                                                                                      2003042563

Book and Jacket Design by
Designs on You!
Suzanna M.W. Stephens

Published by:

Jesse Stuart Foundation
1645 Winchester Avenue • P.O. Box 669
Ashland, Kentucky 41105
(606) 326-1667
JSFBOOKS.com

# Table of Contents

Foreword

Tragedy on Greasy Ridge ................................................ 25

Hardwood Heroes—The Waterloo Wonders ................. 41

Dog Days ........................................................................ 57

Murder on Greasy Ridge ............................................... 65

Elijah's Funeral ............................................................. 79

Reunion at Stony Point ................................................. 85

Mail Pouch ..................................................................... 91

A Tombstone for Simon Davis ....................................... 99

Dark Bluff—The History of an Ohio River Village ........ 103

Graveyard ....................................................................... 119

The Way We Laughed ..................................................... 125

White Whiskey ................................................................ 133

Making Melancholia ........................................................ 151

Moonshine Reflections ................................................... 155

The Story of Bevo Francis .............................................. 169

Clyde Raymond Beatty ................................................... 191

Revival ............................................................................ 203

Foggy Riffs ..................................................................... 211

*Danny Fulks*

# Acknowledgements

*∞◯∞*

These essays have been updated, edited, and, in most cases, protracted from the original publications. Used by permission. Other stories are new.

Fulks, Danny G.

"Making Melancholia," *Now And Then*, Vol.12, No. 2 (Summer, 1995) Copyright Center For Appalachian Studies, ETSU; and *The MacGuffin*, Vol. 15, No. 4. (Spring, 1998).

"The Way We Laughed," *Now And Then*, Vol. 14, No. 1 (Spring, 1997) Copyright Center For Appalachian Studies, ETSU.

"Hardwood Heroes—The Waterloo Wonders," Timeline, Vol. 5, No. 1. (February - March, 1988).

"Moonshine Reflections," *Timeline*, Vol. 7, No. 3. (June - July, 1990).

"The Story of Bevo Francis," *Timeline*, Vol. 9, No. 1. (February - March, 1992).

"Dark Bluff," *Timeline*, Vol. 11, No. 6. (November - December, 1994).

"Mail Pouch," *Timeline*, Vol. 13, No. 4. (July - August, 1996).

"Murder On Greasy Ridge," *Tales Along The Appalachian Plateau*, Huron, Ohio, Bottom Dog Press, 1995, and the Dayton, Ohio *Sunday News Magazine*. (November 30, 1986).

"Reunion At Stony Point," *Tales Along The Appalachian Plateau*, Huron, Ohio, Bottom Dog Press, 1995.

"Graveyard," *Tales Along The Appalachian Plateau*, Huron, Ohio, Bottom Dog Press, 1995.

"Clyde Raymond Beatty," *Timeline*, Vol. 19, No. 4. (July - August, 2002).

*The author's parents,
Grover and Flossie Fulks.
Fulks was also Momma's
maiden name.*

# Foreword

The circle of my experiences growing up in the 1930s and '40s in Gallia County, Ohio, was small. A two-mile ride over the hill to Crown City. Once or twice a year to Huntington, West Virginia. Now and then to Ironton or Gallipolis, Ohio. Too young to help out in the fields of corn, tobacco, and hay, or to help with the cows and hogs, we played nearby in the creeks or carried water to the farm hands. We made paths through the fields of corn that lasted all summer and took us to the rock houses, grapevine swings, and hillsides where ground squirrels darted about, and where the killdeers sang their mournful songs. On Sundays and through big meetings where preaching, singing, and saving souls went on nightly for two weeks in the summers, we watched and listened as sermons of grace were brought forth by old men in galluses, garter sleeves, and white shirts soaked with sweat. We saw old women shout and wave their handkerchiefs in the air. We heard the sweet singing of the choirs, adults praying in unison, and sinners begging to be saved. We chased one another around the church grounds, went off to drink cool spring water, and ate at the long rough-hewn table set with food at the all-day meeting called homecoming.

My dad and I traipsed up the road one day to see John Belville's dead body lying in the dirt of his barn floor. He had hung himself, and neighbors had already taken his body down. The undertaker went through his pockets and, making sure others saw him, turned John's effects over to a family member. The men carried his body down the hill and put it in the back of a hearse. When a person died, we went to the houses of family members and neighbors as the old folks sat up all night in living rooms where bodies lay in repose in cheap coffins. Women fainted in front of their beloved dead as they looked upon, and often caressed, the corpse's face. The dead in their coffins were lowered into the red clay by ropes held by two men on each side of the grave, forever to rest beside other bodies and George Odell's leg. My mother cut fresh roses from trellises, put them in quart jars of water, and left them on the graves of family members who had gone on to heaven. It was called Decoration Day and, if our parents had small change, we stopped at the store for ice cream as the warm May sun softened the asphalt on paved roads. When we went to school, we heard the teacher say that Rosemary would be out for a few days; her mother had died. We hoped our mothers would never die.

We lived among milk cows, hogs, chickens, and work horses. We milked cows by hand, sending silky streams of milk squirting into galvanized buckets. We called in horses, harnessed and hooked them to singletrees for pulling plows, sleds, and wagons, sometimes even struggling and heaving to pull a car out of the ditch. We rode the horses off to distant fields, their sweat stinging our legs through bibbed overalls. Chickens ran loose. We gathered eggs from bushel baskets hung inside cribs and barns. We watched our mothers take a dozen eggs, mark them with pencils, and leave them in a nest for a sitting hen. We traded grown pullets to the rolling store peddler for sugar, lard, salt, and cereals. We saved enough to kill and serve up for Sunday dinners. We took the leftovers to school the next day in a lard bucket. When the ground thawed in March, the barn yard became a mud hole. In summer, we played barefooted in the pastures, stepping in fresh cow droppings that oozed up between our toes.

Christians that we were, we never worked on Sundays except to milk. The scripture told us it was all right to get the ox out of the ditch, even on the Sabbath. It was also good and righteous for the women to cook up a big Sunday dinner on a wood stove in the kitchen. We were never away from home overnight; cows had to be milked 365 days. We went to Gallipolis, located on the Ohio River north of Hun-

*Sharon Lester, Walter Eanes, Brenda Jude, Charles Eanes, 1956. Easter Sunday morning in southern West Virginia coal country.*

tington, West Virginia, each month to pick up feed, pay taxes, and loaf on the Saturday sidewalks. Dad traveled to Maysville, Kentucky, once a year to sell our tobacco. When the tobacco money came in, we had a few extra things for Christmas: toys for us, and oysters for Christmas dinner. The rest went to pay interest on personal notes. When my baby brother died at eighteen months, five years before I was born, my dad used the tobacco money to pay off the undertaker.

The seasons came and went, bringing their own riffs. The conflict with nature never let up. Long, dreary winters began in November and continued through March. Short days, cloudy skies, rain, snow, sleet, and hail cast their own bleakness on the land and its people. We hauled coal in with horses and wagons, piled it in the barnyard, and carried it into the house and outbuildings one bucket at a time. We cut wood for kindling from logs and gathered it from the woods. We slept in cold bedrooms under homemade comforts while the banked coal in the fireplace settled into ashes only to be stirred up again early the next morning. No one ever slept in unless they took sick. We took manure out of the cowbarn each day after the morning milking. The sadness of winter and graves covered with snow was seldom given over to joy. My mother rubbed our chests with kerosene and melted salve in a spoon held over the chimney of a coal oil lamp when we had colds or flu. On better days we skated on the frozen creeks, listened to Jack Armstrong on a battery radio, and wondered at the smell of skunk that was usually on someone's clothes. Summers expanded the chances for play with sunny days, more daylight, and outside events. Much of the melancholy dissipated. But nature continued to try to take everything. We cut brush, grubbed out new ground, fought copperheads, and struck back at poison ivy vines. The trees along the pastures and fields dropped seeds, trying to swallow up the cleared land. We chopped weeds from the garden and the fields. We cut redbrush that grew along the creeks with mowing scythes until the winds and waters of fall scattered seeds to the winds and waters, where they floated away toward the Ohio.

*The author's grandpa, James Fulks, left, builds a house along Indian Guyan Creek, circa 1914. Amenities included an ice house where ice, cut from the creek in winter, was stored for summer. He and his wife, Buena Vista, named for a Civil War battleground, had seven children all of whom lived into their nineties. James, aged 60, was killed in a fight with Banks Dillon in 1922. Dillon was convicted of second degree murder, served five years in the West Virginia State penitentiary in Moundsville.*

We strung everything together with words. There were always voices in the background. The pace of life was such that the people we knew talked freely among one another. We talked while we did the boring, dirty, hard work that left us smelling like stale sweat, our blisters and scrapes stinging. A person might break out in song with a few verses of a hymn or a bluegrass tune but there were no harmonies, no groups swinging to and fro as the poor were shown in the movies. There were a few family secrets, but we did not play roles and most things in life were laid bare without shame. Talk was prized. It was said that certain people were good talkers. Sometimes people had "words." Or you might get a "talking to." Maybe "talked into" something. Christian women did not talk dirty and, especially, did not take the Lord's name in vain. The common dirty words from ancient cultures of the West were spoken, however, by men and boys. Not in front of women. I saw a man who had served time in state prison for a felony chastise a person who blackguarded in front of some women in a country store. She, a person who called bulls gentleman cows. Children talked, too. They listened and were in on everything. There was a security and a hedge against loneliness and fear in hearing grownups talk. We drifted off to sleep as the rhythmic voices, some still carrying an old world brogue, came from the men and women talking into the night. They talked of politics, wars, old times, and the small events of the day. They gossiped about family and neighbors. After long discussions, when someone left to go home, they retold the stories from the different points of view that person's absence opened up. They talked about who had the best tobacco crops, how many jars of green beans had come up; of trials going on in town for persons they knew who had been caught stealing chickens; of funny things that happened like Max McGuire driving his Model A Ford on the rim all the way to Crown City, sparks flying from the gravel as he passed; of stupid kids who poured molasses into their hair or jumped up and down trying to make a cake in the oven sink down. Neighbors passing by in cars and driving teams of horses would stop along the road in front of the house and talk as dad leaned in the car window. A man who lived up the creek from us drug the battery off his car on a rock and drove on several miles until his car quit. Another person stopped and told Dad he had just bought this car, said he didn't know what make it was. Dad went around front, looked, and told him it was a Chrysler. They talked while smoking roll-your-owns and chewing homemade twists mixed with plugs of Star wrapped neatly with shiny metal stars shoved into them.

Most of the people who took dinner with us were either family members, field hands, sellers of Raleigh products, or feed salesmen who happened to show up at dinner time. But anyone who was there at meal time ate. And talked. Pie or cake for dessert? Why, both. Wherever we gathered there was talk: in the country stores, outside the church houses, in town on the sidewalks of Gallipolis; in the fields, in the cow barns, in cars as we rode down the highways; at the townhouse when the trustees met, or on election days; inside school auditoriums where basketball was king and giving the preachers fits because they played on church nights. We talked in beer joints, and in front of coal banks where coal was loaded into wagons. We were alike: white, mostly Republican, and Protestant. Yet we were different. Some were bullies who would run their cows into a neighbor's pasture field and threaten to kill him if he brought it up. Others were drifters who were always looking for a family to take them in for what work they could get out of them. There were thieves, men who hid inside fodder shocks after visiting a neighbor's wife, and people who sold blind horses to the helpless and ignorant, people too dumb to go to hell. Elections were stolen as crooked clerks counted certain candidates out. Losers of school board elections burnt school houses down. People sold teaching jobs to the highest bidders. Teachers taught on certificates taken by smarter people who gave fake names when they took the test.

Most people in the community valued their good names. Everyone knew who they were. If a person's words were no good in a deal, if he squealed out of an agreement, if he worked on Sunday, everyone in the community knew about it. But they understood capitalism. If people could sell a piece of ground or a milk cow for more than it was worth, good for them. Skinning someone without lying or scheming was not a sin, and besides they believed in once-in-grace, always-in-grace. All but the most skeptical were fatalists, anyway. They were heirs to the theology of Old Primitive Baptism. God was in control. Whether events went for or against them, they accepted the good as gifts from God and the bad as a lesson learned. It was in the Sunday hymns: they sang of having a new life over yonder, flying away, walking the last mile, being in the roll call in heaven, the land where no one grows old, meeting all in the morning, and gathering buds from the master's bouquet. Fitting phrases and riffs for people who lost infants to death and were present when the old folks died. Songs that reflected a nature that could not be controlled, only adapted to and held back for awhile by love, home remedies, wood, fire, water, and primitive shelters. They knew hard times, but a mansion waited just over the hilltop. Leave it to the big city fools who didn't even believe in God to try to control events through science and invention. The secular music played in beer joints, school houses, and on back porches was of the same themes: there were men of constant sorrow, graves on green hillsides, tragic romances, and kids who died in their sleep after being made to go to bed. They sang, prayed, talked, and lived sadness. In strawberry patches on sandy hillsides, men and women chopping their way through dirt and weeds would sing out a few verses of the sinking of the Titanic or the death of Floyd Collins. But there were those times when joy prevailed. They had their weddings, bellings, new babies to make over, family dinners, trips to the county fair, sports, shade trees, and the exquisite experiences of youth before the pains of cynicism and separation came.

Stories of great events drifted down through the years. My mother clipped stories from newspapers that she pulled out on winter nights. They were yellow, faded, and worn. They were not really preserved for the ages, just thrown in an old cigar box. There was the story of Faith Massie from a tabloid called the Columbus Star. Faith was a young school teacher who lived up the road and out Greasy Ridge, maybe four miles from our house. She had a bachelor's degree from Ohio University and had taken a job in the fall of 1935 at Tagg School. She could live at home. But on a hot summer weekend before school started, her lover crushed her head with an ore pick, then shot himself. Two children found their bodies lying across a large set of scales used to weigh tobacco and feed. That this could happen on a sleepy, Sunday afternoon while June bugs buzzed around ironweed blossoms still leaves folks bewildered. Mother told us about watching from the front porch as dozens of cars, expresses, and buggies passed on their way to the funeral. Even more bewildering was the 1915 triple murder on the same ridge. Three people killed by their hired hand. Oddly enough, this gruesome crime also happened on Greasy Ridge and the victims were Massies. A mother and her grown son and daughter who lived with her were found many hours after their throats had been cut with a razor. Buzzards had clawed away at their faces and hands. The killer, 18-year-old Harley Beard, took a train to Chicago where one of his sisters lived. He was caught, tried, convicted, and killed in Ohio's electric chair in Columbus seven months later. Carter Massie, then a child, remembered standing in his parent's yard as three horse-drawn hearses passed on their way to the Old Baptist Church. The Massies, along with Faith, lie there still in the graveyard. Their graves are marked with good tombstones, a sign the families had some money. There are still old people in Lawrence County who can dig out the old newspapers, one with the headline: *Ape Man Kills Three On Greasy Ridge.*

Among people who were seldom able to rise above getting by, feats in sports live on still. Waterloo, Ohio, lies about 12 miles from my family's farm, near Greasy Ridge. In 1935 a new basketball coach named Magellen Hairston came to town. He recruited a ragtag group of country boys for the squad. A sportswriter named them the Waterloo Wonders, a name that lives on in the annals of basketball. The wonders played the season without losing a game. They amazed crowds of fans wherever they played. Behind the back passes the length of the court, shooting baskets for their opponents, eating popcorn in the stands as three men controlled the game, smoking Camels as a regular regimen, and making layups so fast their opponents couldn't even see the ball were routine for the Wonders. In the spring, they swept the county and regional tournaments, and went on to win the state competition among teams of their class. The following year they did it all over again playing all over the state, once arriving in Cleveland through a snow storm near midnight to find a gymnasium full of people waiting. They won the state tournament again, and four of the players went on to play professional ball against the outstanding teams in 1940: The Philadelphia Spahs, the Harlem Renaissance, The New York Celtics, and the House of David. They beat the Celtics in a widely acclaimed game at Cleveland's Public Hall in 1936. They played alongside of the greats of the era: Goose Tatum, Sweetwater Clifton, Dutch Dehnert, and Wee Willie Smith. There is still talk that a movie will finally tell their story. In those times, and for years afterward, talk of sports in this region and throughout Ohio always included tales and myths about the fabulous Waterloo Wonders. Their story is on file at the national Basketball Hall Of Fame and is updated from time to time in Sports Illustrated magazine. Five country boys, one coach who beat the odds of poverty, provincialism, petty politics, and the gloom of the Great Depression.

When I enrolled in Rio Grande College in the fall of 1951, among the students I met were two who would become a part of basketball history. I played poker and drank beer with Wayne Wiseman, went to class with the more serious Roy Moses. I dropped out of school the next year and joined the Air Force to avoid the Army as the Korean War was winding down. One day in 1953, inside a cool movie theater in Dallas, Texas, I found Rio Grande's basketball team making the movie newsreels. In the fall of 1952, Newt Oliver came to Rio Grande to coach basketball, bringing with him the six-foot, nine-inch Bevo Francis, a high school star from Wellsville, Ohio. When Oliver assembled his squad, his opening speech was to tell them they were going all the way to stardom in collegiate basketball. Wayne Wiseman laughed. When the team went on the road, however, people began to take notice as they were perfect through the Christmas break. Then, early in 1953 in a home game with Ashland Community College, Bevo scored 116 points himself, 55 coming in the last quarter. The national media took notice, and Rio Grande went on to win every game for the season. The NCAA, after a special session on Bevo and Rio Grande, threw out the record on charges that scores against community and business colleges were unworthy. The ruling was made after the fact, vexing Oliver and thousands of Bevo's fans. The next year Oliver booked games with big basketball powers including Wake Forest and the University of Miami, whipping both. In a game with four-year college, Hillsdale of Michigan, played in Jackson, Ohio, in 1954, Bevo did it again. He scored 113 points, a record that still stands. After the second season, Rio Grande administrators, too petty to realize his worth, expelled Bevo claiming falsely that he had flunked out. He and Oliver signed with the Harlem Globetrotters, Oliver coaching and Bevo playing with the Boston Whirlwinds, a team that traveled with the Globetrotters to provide opposition. When I came back to Rio Grande in the fall of 1954, I roomed with a starter on the Oliver team, Jim McKenzie. Jim taught me a few chords on the guitar, and he and I, after downing a few cold longnecks, attempted to sing and play in a variety show in Rio Grande's Community Hall. Jim passed out before the show and I, backed up by two girls singing doo-ops to *A White Sport Coat And A Pink Carnation,* went on by myself. There were no encores. In 1994, Christopher Duckworth, editor of Timeline Magazine, asked me to write the story, "Bevo's Odyssey." During this time I met Bevo himself.

In *Dark Bluff* I told the story of my hometown, Crown City, how it grew as a typical Ohio River village where steamboats came in and out from New Orleans, Pittsburgh, and points in between. In its time, the early years of the 20th century, it was a lot like Mark Twain's Hannibal, Missouri. Twain said the mornings in Hannibal were spent in anticipation of the boats that put in and the afternoons in dealing with the people and goods they brought. River towns were raucous, filled with outsiders coming in and out, and the mingling of mores. Crown City had its share of hustlers, drinkers, brawlers, and crooks. Some villagers threw rocks at the black roustabouts who worked on the boats if they tried to get off and come ashore. I was born two miles away over the hill from the river. In high school at Mercerville, the two cultures came together. The boys and girls who grew up on the river had wider points of view and experiences. They knew how to set trot lines, boat, and swim. They lived on better land and better roads that took them to town faster and more often.

*Hazel and Barbara Smith, sisters, circa 1950. They are pictured here on their family's 64-acre farm, Kerr Station, Gallia County, Ohio. Their ancestors came there about 1880, originally from Virginia. Barbara's son, Christian, is now a teacher in the Gallipolis City schools.*

*In the picture at right, Alexander Smith, circa 1940, Hazel and Barbara's father. He grew tobacco, corn, and vegetables on his farm.*

Moonshine whiskey and bootlegging were activities that, legal or not, figured into the structure of our social and economic lives. We did not think it was wrong to make and sell whiskey. What was it any business of the government anyway? The Seagrams company could distill and sell whiskey in government stores. Good enough for big shots, against the law for poor folks. Homemade whiskey was a natural product made from corn and yeast, brewed in copper, nothing added. Kernels of corn soaked in warm water for several days causing fermentation. But it was a slow process, a craft. When prohibition came, whiskey was worth more and the demand was so great moonshiners looked for ways to speed up the process. Add sugar. Maybe a dead rat or two. Crooks got in on the business. Then came real trouble. Federal inspectors chased them back then just like they chase weed growers today. In the essay, *Moonshine Reflections,* I drew from stories taken from interviews with former whiskey makers, oral history and scholarly documents. Those I knew were just like anyone else in the community, except they made their own and, perhaps, sold bootleg stuff. It was just a matter of providing a service. Why make someone drive to Ironton to get a pint of Old Crow when you could keep a dozen on hand in Scottown? What is the difference in drinking homemade whiskey and regulated whiskey? Well, the difference is the government doesn't get its part when it's done undercover. Is there a moral difference? People living in the hollows and on the ridges never did like the government that well, anyway. But they did embrace Roosevelt's Work Progress Administration, rural electricity, money for not growing tobacco, and they went to school on the GI Bill. They even signed up for rocking chair money while they waited for school to start. For the story of moonshining and drinking in a larger, historical context, see the essay called *White Whiskey.* Making home brew and whiskey did not start in Ireland, but it was perfected there and brought here by our ancestors.

The essay, *Mail Pouch,* gave me a chance to tell readers, not just about the history of the rustic signs, but also how tobacco was woven into the social fabric. Barns, moreover, were not just places to cure tobacco and strip it into grades called tips, lugs, brightleaf, redleaf, and trash. They were social centers where men gathered to trade knives, swap stories, drink, and talk. Barns were play areas for children. We climbed up and hung from tierpoles, threw rotten eggs, chased wasps, jumped over hay bales, smoked, and showed off black snakes we had killed and drug in from the weeds.

The personal essays in this collection—*Dog Days, The Way We Laughed, Making Melancholia, Graveyard, A Tombstone For Simon Davis, Revival,* and *Reunion At Stony Point*—show that life in northern Appalachia had much in common with life in the south and central Appalachia. The music made was traditional, close to the roots of gospel and bluegrass. More likely to be made on guitars and fiddles; less likely to be from pianos and cellos. Songs of the Carter Family from Poor Valley, Virginia, permeated the land. The Grande Ole Opry from Nashville was a hit with folks who had radios. During and after World War Two, when hillbilly musicians were venturing farther out from southern cities, professional pickers booked shows in school auditoriums singing their latest hits and selling songbooks. In high school, as the young folks began dating, many felt popular singers like Perry Como, Frank Sinatra, Johnny Ray, and Frankie Layne were more romantic. What girl would want to listen to the rags and breakdowns of the Delmore Brothers or Flatt and Scruggs? And how could a banjo provide dance music smooth enough for slow dances? It was almost as if we knew Elvis Presley was strutting around Hume High School in Memphis in pink and black. It wasn't until the folk revival of the sixties when Doc Watson, Joan Baez, and Bob Dylan came along that rural folks began to understand the art of their heritage. It was the same with food. Pinto beans, smoked hams, potatoes, eggs, sausage, and a variety of home grown vegetables were turned into fine meals by our mothers who were, in fact, folk artists who made the bland sublime. Later, traveling in the south, I found the same dishes on menus in mom-and-pop restaurants. After marriage and a family of my own, we were drawn to the South for vacations. Still poor, we went to Florida in the summertime. We took to grits and okra just like we had been eating them for years. And who didn't make an annual pilgrimage to Myrtle Beach, South Carolina? Religion was no different. We liked loud preaching, saving souls, sad hymns, and water baptisms in murky creeks. Just like Alabama. When my family and I finally joined a big-city church we adapted to the indoor baptistry, newsletters, circles of concern where the host served beer, and the lack of women shouting. These essays gave me freedom to wander back to the old-time revivals, burials, all-day meetings with dinners on the ground, family joys and sorrows, characters who wandered by, work, play, the climate, and mundane events that were our sacred rituals.

*White Whiskey* tells the story of homemade whiskey from the early days of the United States into the twentieth century. It is an overview of the broad subject that pitted the wets of large cities against the drys of the church and rural areas. In the background, I try to tell about the political and religious movements that pushed the country to outlaw alcohol only to restore its legality a few years later.

Clyde Beatty, the famous trainer of circus lions and tigers was born in Appalachia near Chillicothe, Ohio, in the village of Bainbridge. Shows how dumb I am. I had long heard of Beatty in the 1940s and 50s, but until Christopher Duckworth, *Timeline* editor, put me on this story, I had no idea where he was from. Not to use superlatives, but it is a super-duper story. You have heard of young boys leaving home and joining the circus. That's what Beatty did, in 1920. He went on to become friends with the rich and famous of his time: Ernest Hemingway, John Wayne, Ed Sullivan, Jack Paar, Mickey Spillane, Pat O'Brien, and Jack Dempsey, among others. His act, caged up with 40 lions and tigers, was the thrill of a nation during World War II. He traveled the world, seeking knowledge and unspoiled cats for his show. He made movies, wrote books, sold cars for Studebaker, and nearly died several times in entanglements with a big cat. Beatty's story is told here. Clyde Beatty is another famous person usually left out of Appalachian stories.

These times have passed. Electricity came in 1939. The WPA brought jobs and better roads. World War II brought sacrifices, fear, and money. Men from the hills shipped off to Europe, Asia, and other faraway lands. As young men left Gallia County, most for the first time, they were filled with excitement and looked forward to the adventure. Old folks cried when their boys left home; but these young men found new places, money, jukeboxes, dirty dancing, poker games, movies, free uniforms, and steam-heated housing were pretty good. Many saw rough times later as they moved toward the front lines. A few were killed, brought back, and buried after ceremonies by the Veterans Of Foreign Wars—their wives or mothers going home with folded flags. But most were through with spending lifetimes in poverty and hard work. Back as far as the early 1900s, now and then, young men went north to work in Ross County, Ohio, saved their money, and came back. They went to the Louisiana bayous to cut timber. Same deal. But World War II changed everything. The men had seen the great cities and the times were good. They jumped on the GI Bill of Rights which paid college expenses for people who never dreamed of getting an education. When they went to college they were able to get along well with blacks, Asians, persons from any ethnic or religious background. They had ridden on half-tracks, flown in airplanes, eaten, drunk, and lived with them in the Army. The 1950s brought television sets, good cars, better roads, Elvis Presley, birth control pills, jet airplanes, bolder movies, Holiday Inns, McDonald's, peace, cheap houses, telephones, refrigerators, Playboy magazine, Rosa Parks, and Sputnik. Again, youth went north. To Cleveland, Dayton, Detroit, and Columbus. Columbus was the first choice. It was just up Routes 35 and 23. Jobs paying 100 dollars a week or more were easy to find. We bragged about our modern houses bought on cheap interest. We learned to merge into the freeways, get around in the big city. We found beer joints on High Street in Columbus where we could hear bluegrass and drink longnecks. Every Friday night, we came back home for the weekend, turned around and went right back on Sunday night. There were always long lines of traffic coming down and going back. Car license plates told of the Kentuckians who were in on the migration. Children were born and, finally, most of us found homes outside the lonely hills. There would be no coming back for good. The farms we left were sold to strip miners; the old home places torn down or reclaimed by nature. The family graveyards grew up in brush, abandoned. After the coal miners and small farmers left, city dwellers from Gallipolis and Huntington, looking to get away from people, bought up land and weekend retreats. A new type of resident took to some on the forlorn places: weed growers, many of whom drew some kind of government checks. We adapted to the cities and liked it there, wanted our children to have the advantages of better schools, and progress. The land we left remained. But it, too, evolved. You can drive out Greasy Ridge and see new houses where people who work in the cities live. Scottown, Crown City, Proctorville. Same thing. Good cars, good roads, an easy drive to work and back.

The past looks better. To keep us from going crazy, our minds filter out bad times. The good times stay with us. Painful experiences from the past dissipate, and we cannot feel them again even when we try. We are not the same people we were then. If you look at your old high school yearbook picture, you will find that person no longer exists. That person's parents were living, education was incomplete, children were unborn. The heartbreaking teenage love affairs are as mist in the evening sunset. Mother's raspberry cobblers never really tasted that good, anyway. We hardly ever go back to visit graves; the grandchildren have their own lives on soccer fields in distant cities. We don't keep a weekend cabin in the woods, too much vandalism, and the kids hate bugs. We don't worry that much about going to hell when we die.

# Tragedy on Greasy Ridge

Mellow light from an orange moon left eerie shadows on the trail. Traveling in the soft dirt path left by wagons and cars, a bay mare and her rider made their way north along Greasy Ridge in Lawrence County, Ohio. Hurrying now down the hill into Lecta, they crossed a wooden bridge, paced their way through the valley past Sand Fork, over another bridge, then up Hannan Trace and Patriot roads, turning the bend toward Centenary. Chickens roosting in trees stirred as the rider pulled back on the reins, slowing down as they crossed the Chickamauga Bridge to Orville Sheets's Livery Stable in Gallipolis. The rider—red-faced, nervous, bushy hair clinging to his low forehead—got Sheets out of bed, stabled the horse, and lay down in a spare bedroom. Long past midnight, Harley Beard had been on the road five hours. Sleep didn't come. Telling Sheets someone would pick up the horse, Beard headed uptown to the Hocking Valley Railroad Station and caught the morning train to Chicago. The next day, Friday, May 14, 1914, Beard, an 18-year old itinerant farm hand, found food and shelter at his sister Viola Davis's house on West Madison Street. Beard didn't know it, but the next day his name and picture would appear at the top of page one, *Chicago Daily Tribune,* inside the pages of the *New York Times,* and on the front pages of Ohio's major papers. Nor did he know that seven months later, on a cold December night, he would enter the Palace Of Death, Ohio Penitentiary, Columbus, and die there in the electric chair as Lawrence County Sheriff Glen Sloan, Warden Preston Thomas, and others looked on.

As the sun came up Friday morning on Greasy Ridge, crows were on the wing, tender wild daisies broke through borders around the

No. 44 Harley Beard
Of Lawrence County. Electrocuted December 4, 1914, for the Murder of Bob-Mary-Nancy Massie.

*Harley Beard's prison photo. Like the song goes, "They called him by a number not a name, Lord, Lord"—42857-102.*

flats, and white violets nested in the damp woods. John Clary was up and dressed, planning a long day in the fields getting the hillside flats and ridge newground ready for spring planting. His neighbor, 49-year-old Robert Massie, Mason Township Treasurer, had offered earlier to lend Clary a harrow. Leading a work horse, he walked into the field to pick it up. Finding the harrow's double-tree missing, he walked on toward the Massie house. A dog barked and walked back and forth near the summer kitchen where Robert slept. Clary had walked into the Massie yard many times before, and, other than the barking dog, there was no sign that anything was wrong. But as he approached the house, he saw Robert sprawled face down, his head crushed, flesh torn from his face by buzzards. Clary turned away in shock, and ran out the ridge yelling for the closest neighbor, Ulysses Dennison. As Dennison's wife alerted others, he and Clary returned to the scene. Inside the house, they found Robert's 78-year-old mother, Nancy, lying in the middle of the dining room floor, her throat cut, her skull crushed. And on the kitchen floor lay Robert's 47-year-old sister, Mary, her hands tied across her breast with bailing twine. She, too, was dead, her throat slashed.

The three had been dead for two days. News of this macabre incident traveled through Mason Township to Ironton, Gallipolis, and the surrounding area. Glenn Sloan, Detective John King, and Coroner Oliver O'Neill motored out from Ironton. A bloody shirt and pants, a razor, a heavy, iron-banded device used to hold hay bales together, and a set of bloody clothes were among the items recovered. Mary Massie's riding mare and Harley Beard's Sunday clothes were gone. In a telephone conversation with law officers in Gallipolis, Sloan found that a young man had left a horse there and boarded a Chicago-bound train. Sam Davis, a Greasy Ridge farmer and father-in-law to Beard's sister, Viola, gave authorities the Chicago address. Glen Sloan, a respected man of the law, was on the chase, and Beard, who had wound up on Greasy Ridge after drifting among a host of relatives, was on the lam.

Harley Beard, one of eight children from the family of Elizabeth and Arthur Beard, was born in Franklin, Ohio, in 1896. When his mother died in 1904, the family was separated and he was sent to the Morrow County Children's Home. He later lived with his father and stepmother. When his father died in 1909, the 14-year-old Beard lived for a year with a sister in Middletown, Ohio, before moving to Chicago to live with Viola. In July 1913, he came to Greasy Ridge to work on Sam Davis's farm. Beard, slight of build, weighing 118 pounds, took to the steady rhythm of life there, did odd jobs, and went to Sunday school at the Old Regular Baptist Church. There were good times: watching the pinhookers buy and sell tobacco in the Rappsburg warehouse, buying roll-your-owns at John Heidorn's Grocery, standing at the back of crowds gathered for bellings, and watching softball games at Tagg School. September came. Robert Massie—cattle buyer, farmer, and trader—needed help. Harley Beard was available, and for five dollars a week cash money, room with breakfast, dinner, and supper, he moved in with the Massies to do odd jobs, work in the garden, hoe tobacco, and feed hogs. He and the Massies took in tobacco, tied it for market, and cared for livestock. The winter passed. Greasy Ridge was silent except for the sounds of leather harness straps slapping against work horses, the calls of killdeer, and the screeches of hoot owls. The

Phyllis Clary collection

*Tagg Road near Greasy Ridge Road—1904. Row 1, left to right: Charles, Mary, John, Ora, Oyer Clary. Row 2, left to right: Charlie Tagg, his sister Cora Myers, Oathe Massie. John Clary found the bodies of the Massie family.*

township constable took care of fights, drunks, and bootleggers.

Glenn Sloan made his move late on Friday. He and Albert Merriman, Gallia County Prosecutor, wired Beard's description and Viola's address to the Chicago Police Department. The police found him there, arrested him, confiscated a gold watch and $20, and locked him up. Sloan, fearless, made plans to go to Chicago. Beard was talking. He told the Chicago police he had been kicked around a lot in his life and that Robert Massie was a hard man who often cussed and swore at him. He and Mary had quarreled early in the week and she told Robert about it. Robert accused Beard of making romantic advances toward his sister and threatened to cut his head off with a hatchet. As their words became more heated, Beard knocked him in the head. Running into the house, Mary grabbed Beard. He knocked her down, then Nancy. Hearing the two women moaning, he panicked and cut their throats with Sam Davis's razor. Captain Thomas J. Coughlin of the Chicago Police, waiting for Sloan to arrive, asked Dr. Harold N. Moyer, head of the department's psychopathic division, to examine Beard. Moyer diagnosed him as an irresponsible degenerate, a low-grade moron, or, at best, an imbecile. Among the tests Moyer used was one where a pin was stuck into Beard's forehead. When he asked him if it hurt, Beard told him he didn't know what he was talking about. He flunked what was called the memory span, repeating a series of out-of-order numerals. Moyer said it took his patient 25 seconds to have an idea, that he was suffering from a deteriorated mentality. His mental age was 10, and the doctor saw no evidence that he would develop further.

While Beard was being interrogated in the Cook County jail, the train carrying Glen Sloan rolled north along steel rails to Chicago. There, as evening shadows cut through skyscrapers on Michigan Avenue and early evening moviegoers lined up to see newsreels from the battle of Vera Cruz, Sloan's quarry sat emotionless behind bars, ready and willing to go back to Ironton. On the southbound train, Beard was amazed that so many people recognized him from pictures in newspapers. When Sloan asked him why he killed the whole family, Beard said he didn't know why, he just got mad and didn't know what he was doing; that after he hit Robert, he went into the house to finish a Dickens novel, *Nicholas Nickleby*. Beard told Sloan the same story he gave to the Chicago police. He laughed, telling about overhearing another prisoner, jailed for theft, say he had picked up a rope that happened to have a horse on the other end of it. Beard knew enough to figure out he was in trouble. He knew they killed convicted murderers in Ohio, that the electric chair had replaced the noose. He told Sloan he was sorry he did it and wished the Massies were still alive. Sloan, knowing perhaps that Sheriff Jasper Kimball had lost a man to a group of marauders 30 years earlier, assured the uneasy Beard that he would get a fair trial. During a brief stop in Richmond, Indiana, Detective King from Ironton told Sloan by telephone about tensions developing there, especially in Mason Township. Determined not to give in to vigilantes, he got permission from the Scioto County sheriff to drop his prisoner off in Portsmouth, a few miles west of

Ironton. That evening, he was back in Ironton in time to attend the biggest funeral Lawrence County had ever seen.

By mid-morning on Sunday, the May sun had soaked up the night frost on Greasy Ridge. At the Massie house, where the corpses had lain in coffins as family and friends sat up all night, three horse-drawn hearses were backed up to the front door. Directed by James Myers, an undertaker from Sand Fork, 18 pall bearers, three preachers, and a crowd of mourners assembled. The procession moved forward—buggies, Model Ts, motorcycles, wagons, and folks on foot made the two-mile trek along the gravel road to the Old Baptist Church. Constables and deputy sheriffs lined the road, directing traffic, cutting barbed wire fences to make space for horses to graze during the services. The closed coffins were fixed on catafalques near the church altar. Massie relatives filled the pews and more than a thousand people gathered on the grounds. The preachers, led by Walter Shafer and Judge Edward Corn, speaking for the law and relatives of the dead, exhorted all to respect the legal process and not to engage in revenge. There would be no violence against Harley Beard. Shafer and two fellow preachers assured the crowd that heaven with its promise of eternal peace, had claimed the dead. As noon came, men with hats in hand, women in feed-sack dresses, and children in Sunday clothes passed by the coffins. The Massie family was buried, side-by-side, in three open graves on the churchyard knoll. As the crowd dissipated, long evening shadows of hundred-year-old pin oak trees fell across fresh dirt and wilting flowers piled upon the graves. Dust stirred up by cars, horses, and walkers settled on the redbrush growing wild along the ditches.

As Massie relatives and constables turned away strangers and neighbors from the bloody death scene, threats of lynching and smallpox problems in the Portsmouth jail eased. Harley Beard's sister, Maria Knorr, of Newport, Kentucky, came to visit. She and Beard talked for more than an hour. In an interview with a reporter, Maria told about receiving letters from her brother complaining that Robert Massie had

Gallia County Historical Society

*In 1915 blacksmith shops like Hut Roberts' in Waterloo, Ohio, were common.*

cussed him often and worked him 16 hours a day. She said Harley could be as bright as anyone one minute, then do something stupid the next. Maria assured her brother she would be back for the trial.

In Ironton, Edward Corn's special grand jury was ready by Thursday. The 15 jurors listened as Corn told them the crime was unprovoked and unwarranted. Beard would be tried for the killing of Mary Massie, leaving the way open for trials on the other two later if needed. He explained that Beard should be charged with first-degree murder, because the killing of the women was premeditated and that conviction could result in the defendant's execution. There were 13 witnesses, including several relatives of the victims, Sheriff Sloan, John Clary, and Arna Neal, who had been to the Massie farm the day of the murders. Testifying under the guidance of Prosecutor Lindsay Cooper, Neal told that they and Beard had been peacefully setting out sweet potato plants. He was the last person to see the family alive. The next day, Sloan brought Beard up from Portsmouth, gave him a copy of the indictment, and left him in the county jail. Broke and friendless, except for Maria, he accepted his court-appointed attorney, Perry Booth, who entered a guilty plea for his client at the arraignment, declined to request a change of venue, and went along with holding the trial in front of a judge rather than calling a petit jury. This was the first time in the history of Lawrence County that a defendant had pleaded guilty to a charge of first-degree murder. Judge Corn, himself a relative of the Massies, set trial for June 15 and called on Judge James Thomas from Portsmouth to preside. Cooper began collecting evidence and interrogating witnesses against the young man who, according to the *Herald Dispatch* newspaper in Huntington, West Virginia, had a low forehead and eyes peculiarly set close together.

Ironton was still a bustling center of trade even though the blast furnaces of the Hanging Rock iron region had long since passed the glory days when it produced the best pig iron in North America. Like other river towns, hustlers and swindlers intermingled on the low streets with industrious men and women, and an occasional iron baron. The six-year-old Greek Revival Court House topped off with a shiny, copper dome was the pride of the city and the many farmers from places like Linville and Black Fork. Roads, river boats, and railroads converged where Park Avenue took travelers past Wesley Tulga's buggy and harness store over the horizon toward Pedro, Jackson, and Chillicothe. Here in this halcyon place, the most notorious trial in the history of the Ohio Valley was about to take place.

Farmers from Greasy Ridge, Civil War veterans, and reporters were among the hundreds who gathered on the high court house grounds early Monday morning, June 15. As the hot afternoon approached, lawyers in dark suits and officers in uniform led by Court Constable Will Corn blended with the majesty of wide marble stairways, high ceilings, and ornate woodwork. City lawyers, preachers, and doctors had priority seats in the crowded pews as hundreds waited outside, gossiping, and pulling on Fatimas. Judge James Thomas, robed in full

*United States Post Office, Rappsburg, Ohio, circa 1950 with Nancy Stumbo. She and her husband, Alpha, owned the store which, among other items, sold dynamite to coal miners. Scales shown on the right were left out at night. Harley Beard may have bought cigarettes here.*

regalia, walked in as everyone stood. Maria Knorr, in white dress and black hat, entered with Perry Booth. Harley Beard, handcuffed, suited in black, came in with Sheriff Sloan and took a seat on a bench with his sister and Sam Davis. John Clary, the first witness, told his story about finding Robert's body, returning to the scene with Ulysses Dennison, and going into the house where they found the bodies of Nancy and Mary. Clary had not heard of any trouble the family was having with Beard and, from his experience, the defendant was not a hot-headed young man. Elmer Massie, cousin to Robert and Mary, described the imprint of a hand in the blood beside Mary, the positions of the bodies, and their clothing. He identified the club and razor Prosecutor Cooper displayed for the judge. Other witnesses from Greasy Ridge confirmed Beard's pleasant nature, one calling him an "ideal boy," another telling that the defendant called Nancy, "grandma." Ulysses Dennison, however, said he had heard Robert and Mary tease Beard about lying to them. Coroner O'Neill, after a lengthy, deliberate description of details, said the women died from hemorrhages and Robert from two blows to his head. Sheriff Sloan revealed Beard's comments on the train from Chicago that Mary had come into his bedroom on one occasion and that Robert often sassed him. After the bedroom incident, he said Robert had threatened to cut his head off.

Perry Booth called Sam Davis to the stand, and he told his story about Beard coming to live with him the summer of 1913. Beard was a truthful, hard-working boy who went to church and Sunday school, although he was not very smart, according to Davis. Dr. Elmer Wells, an Ironton physician, told the judge that Beard was a young man with a low forehead and normal senses who knew he had committed a heinous crime. When Judge Thomas asked Wells whether Beard's

*The Rappsburg Post Office building in 1990.*

Author's collection

speech problem indicated insanity, he said it did not. Dr. Nathanial Moxley, another Ironton doctor, testified that his examination showed Beard to be sane. He, too, said the defendant's difficulty in speaking plain had nothing to do with his state of mind. Dr. Lester Keller agreed with the other doctors confirming their judgment that Beard was sane. Perry Booth did not present the judge with assessments from the Chicago psychiatrists. After brief questioning of the doctors by Booth, the judge recessed the trial until Tuesday morning.

Courtroom pews filled, principals in place, preliminary rituals performed, and the bailiff Will Corn in charge, Perry Booth put Harley Beard on the witness stand. He reviewed his life story for the court including events leading up to the murders. Answering questions from his lawyer, he told how he killed the family, saying he cut the women's throats because they were groaning and he couldn't stand to hear them go on. When Booth asked him whether he would tell God the same story knowing he might be electrocuted, Beard proclaimed his belief in Heaven and Hell, and that God was watching him as he was killing three people. He showed little emotion as the morning passed, smiling once as he told about Robert being vexed because he was shucking corn uphill. In the afternoon session, Beard told Judge Thomas he had nothing against the two women, but under vigorous questioning he admitted tying Mary's hands with twine thinking she might get to the telephone. Booth asked him to identify the twine and Beard said the blood on it was proof. When he went on to say that Mary had made overtures to him, Elmer Massie, the surviving brother raised up, moving toward Beard and calling him a liar. As the judge hammered his gavel, Roy Massie, a deputy sheriff, and Prosecutor Cooper wrestled Elmer to the floor. Maria Knorr screamed asking for God's mercy. Courtroom visitors stood, many trying to get to the doors as deputies held them back. When order was restored, Beard went on to say that he had struck Robert twice intending to kill him. Unable to get Beard's distraught sister to testify, Booth rested.

Prosecutor Cooper reviewed the case reprising the premeditation charge and the expert testimony against insanity. He called on the judge to sentence Beard to execution for crimes against God and society. Perry Booth did not argue about the sanity issue, but did try to convince the judge that the defendant's low intelligence precluded a scheme of premeditation. Since no credible motive was established, he asked that his client be shown mercy. Cooper again reiterated Beard's confession and opinions of the doctors who spoke to his sanity. Death in the electric chair was the only way to bring justice. Judge Thomas embarked on a long soliloquy about true soldiers never faltering and his profound responsibility to maintain a state of mind consistent with 12 imaginary jurors. He reviewed the indictment, phases of the case, and Beard's need for pity because of a history of neglect. The judge went on to compliment Booth for not pressing to blacken the character of the dead or questioning the chaste nature of Mary Massie's character. "Harley Beard, you may stand up," said Judge Thomas, "What have you to say before sentence is passed upon you?"

"Nothing, only I ask for mercy," Beard replied. When the judge asked the defendant whether he had read in the Bible about the merciful being blessed, he said he hadn't got that far. Declaring that Beard showed no mercy, the judge sentenced him to die in the electric chair, Ohio Penitentiary, on October 2. Maria Knorr cried out in anguish calling Beard her darling brother as those in attendance shuffled across the aisles toward the exits. Sheriff Sloan handcuffed Beard, took him to his cell, and waited for the paperwork required before he could turn him over to Warden Preston Thomas at the Ohio Penitentiary in Columbus where he would take his place among the new prisoners— "fresh fish," in prison jargon.

The rhythm of life on Greasy Ridge, slow and steady as it was, returned as the summer passed. Farmers, merchants, and day laborers kept pace with long, sleepy days watching apples redden, canning peaches, and chopping weeds with goose-neck hoes. Elmer Massie took over the family estate and kept up with events at the penitentiary expecting to witness the execution. Special pleas came in to

Governor James Cox, an opponent of capital punishment, to spare Beard's life because of his age and mentality, arguments made by sentimentalists and breeders of anarchy as far as Elmer Massie was concerned. Cox lost a tough election, against Republican Frank Willis, but he granted Beard a stay of execution on September 28. By postponing the execution 60 days, he was able to get the problem off his desk until after the election.

In early December, the gaiety of Christmas brought shoppers out to stroll past the elegant Neil House on their way to F and R Lazarus's department store on South High Street in Columbus, contrasting with the ominous, Gothic stone Ohio Penitentiary located at the confluence of the Olentangy and Scioto Rivers. Open since 1834, the Ohio Penitentiary was better known as a place where prisoners begged guards not to tie them to a whipping post than a place of rehabilitation. On the evening of December 3, Harley Beard—number 42857-102—was moved to a holding cell near the death chamber in the prison's East Hall. Still hopeful for a reprieve, he had written Governor Cox a letter asking for another chance, saying he didn't know what he was doing when he killed the Massies and reminding him that God was merciful. But with no word coming from the Governor, events

*Ohio State Penitentiary, Columbus, Ohio*

moved inexorably toward midnight. Chaplain Thomas Reed came for prayer and the last meal, promising to pass along Beard's warning to other orphans to stay away from bad company, cigarettes, and alcohol, a statement that was printed on the first page of the *Columbus Dispatch* the next day. He assured those concerned that Beard had accepted Christ and was ready to die. Glenn Sloan arrived from Ironton where, earlier in the day, he had told a disappointed Elmer Massie that the Governor did not want him there. Warden Thomas led the march down the long corridor through East Hall, moving without noise on the sawdust-covered floor. Beard's hair was clipped shortly before midnight and, seated in the electric chair, his ankles, knees, arms, and shoulders were clamped tight. A sponge, soaked in a solution of ammonia and water, was placed on his head and calf, completing the circuit. The Warden asked, "Have you anything to say be-

fore the sentence of the court shall have finally been carried out?" Beard replied, "I do not think it right to send me to my father which is in heaven." At 12:15 a.m., the executioner, forever anonymous, pulled the lever sending 1750 volts into the victim for 75 seconds,

*Electric chair—Ohio Penitentiary*

reducing it to 250 for 45 seconds. Beard's body plunged upward against the clamps, his nails sunk into his flesh, his body stiffened, and his tendons pushed against his skin. Six minutes later, Dr. Orin Kramer pronounced him dead. Viola Day, in from Chicago but not present at the execution, claimed the body. She and her sister, Maria Knorr, took the remains to Newport, Kentucky, for burial. The news of Beard's death spread fast from Columbus to Ironton and into the outlying areas. The semi-weekly *Irontonian* reported that evening that Beard was hard to kill, requiring an extra shock of electricity.

Death was no stranger to the folks who lived on Greasy Ridge. They and their ancestors had been there throughout the nineteenth century. They had lived through the deaths and burials of babies. They had nursed their old at home where most died in their own beds as family members and preachers prayed and, with love, offered companionship. Living in harmony with nature's wrath and its blessings complemented the riffs of a prevailing fatalism. As the Holidays passed, again, they tied and marketed tobacco, cut firewood, dug coal,

*Massie grave and monument, Old Baptist Church graveyard on Greasy Ridge Road, Lawrence County, Ohio.*

cooked on wood stoves, and traipsed off to prayer meetings at the Old Baptist. Spring would come bringing forth new life as cows gave birth to baby calves and the brown of winter would give way to bluebells, green fields, and long sunny days. Bearing witness to the pace of life on Greasy Ridge, John Clary's son, Oyer, died in 2000 when he was 98 and is buried within a half mile of the place where the Massie family was murdered.

*Unidentified person with an expensive car from the Harley Beard era.*

Brenda Koontz collection

# Hardwood Heroes—
# The Waterloo Wonders

In the spacious lobby of the Fort Hayes Hotel in Columbus, patrons milled about. Bell captains and porters in splendid uniforms hustled tips from overnight guests in exchange for help with baggage and other favors. High school basketball coaches and principals from across the state stood about in threes and fours, many of them glumly enduring hangovers—the result of a long night before in the smoky hospitality suites of the sporting goods companies. A scattering of loafers and traveling salesmen lounged in the lobby's overstuffed chairs, smoking cigarettes and reading newspapers. At the dining room cash register, people queued to pay their luncheon checks. One floor down, at the foot of the wide, marble stairway, businessmen, politicians, and lawyers freshened up in the restroom while others sat silently in the long row of shoeshine stalls.

Near the revolving door that led to Spring Street, five young men in black and white satin warm-up jackets stood, waiting for directions from a slightly older man in a dark gray suit. After a brief exchange of words they moved together through the door, walked to a 1935 Ford V-8 sedan, got in, and drove off. They moved with the traffic north on High Street, the tension that had been building for two days mounting as the city blocks passed by. When they turned east onto Eleventh Avenue and approached the Ohio State Fairgrounds, they were on the final leg of a journey into basketball immortality.

They walked toward the fairgrounds coliseum amidst lines of people crisscrossing the adjacent quadrangle. There, surrounded by the blue and white colors of New Matamoras, the red and black of

Blanch Spears collection—plate provided by the Ohio Historical Society

*The Waterloo Wonders after winning the state basketball championship in 1935. Wyman Roberts, Curtis McMahon, Coach Magellan Hairston, Orlyn Roberts, Beryl Drummond, Stewart Wiseman.*

Groveport, the purple and gold of Maumee, and the red, white, and blue of Oxford Stewart, the Waterloo Wonders—Orlyn Roberts, Wyman Roberts, Beryl Drummond, Curtis McMahon, Stewart Wiseman, and their coach, Magellan Hairston—moved toward the arena. They had been in town since Thursday and had already defeated Groveport 39-22 and Fremont St. Joseph 48-21; and they were ready to take on the Oxford Stewart Tigers, whose record for the year stood at 26 and 1.

The Waterloo Wonders were just one victory away from their second straight Class B state high school championship. They were, to the sports fans of Ohio and beyond, already well known. It was March 23, 1935, and 9,000 cheering rooters were squeezed into the coliseum. Even though the Class A championship game between Akron North and Coshocton was also on the program, the excitement of the tournament was focused on the Waterloo game. Inside the cavernous arena, the cheering was intense. Popcorn and soft drink vendors struggled to accommodate the demands for refreshments. Behind the team benches sat radio reporters with live headphones and sports writers with sharpened pencils. The arena announcer prepared to introduce the starting lineups.

The championship game opened with the Tigers controlling the center jump and scoring in the first minute of play. Wyman Roberts of Waterloo countered with a two-hand set-shot from the center line that brought the crowd to its feet. Oxford continued its cool, methodical play. Orlyn Roberts sank a 15-foot hook shot, but Oxford responded with three consecutive goals. The seesaw game continued with Waterloo gaining the jump and tying the game at eight apiece as the first-quarter buzzer sounded. In the second period, Waterloo stepped up the momentum, passing the ball so rapidly that fans found it hard to follow the action. The Wonders moved to their shifting man-to-man defense, and as back-to-back shots by Wyman Roberts and Beryl Drummond fell, the halftime score was 17-13, Waterloo.

> *Black and White, Fight, Fight,*
> *Black and White, Fight, Fight,*
> *Who Fight, We Fight,*
> *Black and White, Fight, Fight*

came the chant from the two Waterloo cheerleaders, dressed in black culottes and heavy black sweaters trimmed in white.

Oxford won the second half tip-off and five seconds later scored from mid-court. Unable to penetrate the Tigers' defense, Waterloo missed six long shots before they again gained control with the Roberts cousins bringing the ball down court with precise behind-the-back passes. But Oxford refused to be intimidated. The Tigers cut Waterloo's edge to 24-20 as the fourth quarter progressed. In the closing minutes, a free throw by McMahon and two by an Oxford player left the final score at 25-22, Waterloo. To the delight of most of the fans who had jammed into the coliseum during the three-day event, Waterloo won a second straight state basketball championship. Only Bellepoint, in 1924 and 1925, had accomplished the feat before. In two seasons of play, the Wonders had won 97 games while losing only three. And many of the games had been against Class A ball clubs and college teams.

Waterloo placed four players on the 1935 all-tournament team, and their 38 percent field-goal shooting was nine points better than Class A champion Akron North's. It was an appropriate climax for the team, and for Orlyn Roberts, who one year earlier had set three enduring records for three-game state tournaments: most points, 69; most field goals, 29; and most free throws, 11. The following day, Sunday the 24th, the most colorful basketball team in the history of Ohio basketball returned in triumph to its native Lawrence County hills.

The character and basketball prowess of the Waterloo Wonders and their coach, Magellan Hairston, were molded in a remote area on the western edge of the Appalachian Plateau. Their lives converged in the village of Waterloo in Lawrence County, home to approximately 150 people in 1935. Located about halfway between Gallipolis and Ironton on State Route 141, Waterloo had maintained a steady growth since being settled in the early nineteenth century. In 1935 the people in the village and the surrounding area, including the smaller villages of Aid, Arabia, Wilgus, Greasy Ridge, Lecta, Cadmus, and Sheritts, furnished business to two doctors and one funeral home; material, social, and spiritual wants were supplied by a post office, an inn, a school, two restaurants, several churches, a general store, a Masonic Hall, a grocery store, and a beer joint. The houses were primarily white, frame dwellings heated by open fireplaces and coal stoves; some had individual Delco generators supplying electricity, and most were connected to the outside world and to each other by a party-line telephone. The residents were white, Protestant, and Republican. It was, strange as it seems, the kind of place that bore and nurtured sports heroes.

The growth of secondary schools in rural America in the 1920s did not bypass Lawrence County. The scattered, two-year academies were gradually replaced by schools that offered a four-year curriculum. The high school at Waterloo was built in 1929, and a gymnasium was added in 1932. In a tradition as old as ancient Greece, physical fitness and competitive sports were incorporated into the education of the youth in rural America.

With the expanding popularity of sports in general, and especially of basketball in the Midwest, the gymnasium began to compete with the church as a social magnet that attracted the young and their parents. Enthusiasm for sports at times took on a religious fervor akin to that of the Chautauqua assemblies and tent revivals; even the typical Wednesday night prayer meetings were muted by the *swoosh* of the basketball through the net. Basketball, played primarily for fun by young men whose main goal was to compete fairly and to entertain the crowds, had become a focus of community pride.

The six protagonists in the odyssey of the Waterloo Wonders were Magellan Hairston, the coach, who at age 26 was a slim young man with an easy smile, a firm handshake, and dark, curly hair; Orlyn Roberts, a 5'11-1/2" master ball handler and showman; Wyman Roberts, a 5'10" forward who seemed to whip the basketball around and between his legs faster than the eyes could follow; Stewart Wiseman, a 5'7" guard from nearby Sheritts who played a watchdog role in the back court; Curtis McMahon, a 5'11" center from Greasy Ridge whose accurate shooting was learned on an outdoor court where missed shots were penalized by a 300-yard roll into a hollow below the barn; and forward Beryl Drummond, a 5'8" transfer student from Cadmus, where he had played second-string ball.

These were the players and their coach who gathered in the high school gym at Waterloo in the fall of 1933. Each of the six men had grown up within 20 miles of the others. The physical and psychological culture of the region was ingrained in each. Early in life they learned the feel of the plow handles, the smell and vitality of the workhorses that supplied the power to turn the soil, and the sweat and calluses born of long hours chopping in the dirt with a gooseneck hoe. They fished and hunted turtles in Symmes, Buckeye, and

Buck creeks; attended backyard rooster fights on long, boring Sunday afternoons. They hunted foxes with dogs through the long nights of autumn, shotgunned for squirrels in the woods, and sold the pelts of raccoons, skunks, and opossums caught in traps and deadfalls along the creeks. They listened to Jack Benny on the radio and to their elders' discussions of FDR's fireside chats. They smoked a few cigarettes and drank an occasional, clandestine beer. Once or twice a year, they traveled to Ironton to take in a movie or shoot pool.

Waterloo started the season of 1933 - 34 without fanfare. They were unknown outside the region, and even the local newspaper, *The Ironton Tribune*, paid little attention to them. Traveling in a black Chevrolet sedan belonging to Hairston, and occasionally by school bus, the Wonders began to test their skills against the local schools. Cadmus, Kitts Hill, Aid-Mason, and Coal Grove were swept away as Waterloo's squad scored an astonishing 290 points while these opponents were held to 57. But it wasn't just the scores that people talked about. By Thanksgiving a unique style of basketball was beginning to show in the Wonders' performances. It had taken the previous year's experience, the new gymnasium, and the addition of Beryl Drummond, but they had integrated their skills and become *the* team to watch in Lawrence County. There they were, night after night—Orlyn Roberts passing behind his back and sometimes even between the legs of opposing guards; Wyman Roberts throwing long passes to McMahon, which he frequently tipped to a third player for the goal; Drummond and Wiseman, both short, screening opponents off the shooters, and all the while Hairston directing from the bench with intensity and determination. They had become the Waterloo Wonders, a name given them by veteran Ironton writer Stan Morris and one that aptly described Lawrence County's Cinderella team.

The Wonders opened the new year of 1934 with wins over Blackford, Pedro, and Racine (Ohio); Russell, Kentucky; and the Marshall College freshmen from Huntington, West Virginia, as they piled up 209 points against 122. The spectacle continued as the Wonders gained crowd approval, confidence, and encouragement for their playing style. They developed a shifting man-to-man defense in which the nearest Wonder closed in on any unguarded opponent until the man assigned was in position to guard his man. The team's unconventional pranks became a hallmark as they learned from experience the crowd-pleasing appeal of their horseplay: getting the tip-off, then handing the ball over to an opposing player and standing clear while he shot; rebounding the missed shot of an opponent and giving him the ball for another try; bouncing the ball off the floor into the basket; and two or three players eating popcorn on the sidelines while the remaining Wonders continued with the game. And on the sidelines at home games, 90-year-old Confederate veteran Perry Brumfield danced jigs to the roars of the crowd.

No area team could touch these Wonders. In the county tournament played at Ironton, teams fell as quickly as the clock could tick off the 32 minutes of play. Chesapeake, Proctorville, Windsor, and Ironton St. Joseph were all turned back in impressive fashion. In the sectional tournament at Gallipolis, Waterloo defeated Cadmus, Hamden, Chesapeake, and Oak Hill, compiling 165 points and holding their opponents to 69. With no sign of weakness, Waterloo defeated Piketon, Highland, and New Boston in the district tournament at Athens. And as the state and region suddenly discovered the Waterloo Wonders, they went on the fairgrounds coliseum court in Columbus and defeated Chandlersville of Muskingum County, Lowellville of Mahoning County, and in the championship game played on March 17, 1934, Mark Center of Defiance. The Waterloo Wonders were state champions and Ohioans took notice.

Waterloo High School opened as usual on the day after Labor Day in the fall of 1934. Coach Hairston and his squad began their daily 45-minute practices in the school gym with the natural enthusiasm of a winning team. These sessions continued until early November brought the beginning of interscholastic competition.

After opening the season with defeats of two local Class B teams,

Wheelersburg and Green Township, the Wonders were scheduled against two highly rated Class A clubs—Columbus Central and Springfield—in their third and fourth games. Departing in early December, they headed north along the familiar, winding highways through Oak Hill, Jackson, Chillicothe, and Circleville to Columbus. They beat Columbus Central 34-25 on a Friday night and the next day traveled to Springfield, 45 miles to the west, where they played to a full house at Tiffany Gym—the score, Waterloo 30, Springfield 19. In beating Springfield the Wonders employed their entire range of skills: they passed sharply, confused their opponents with their floor maneuvers, held the ball for long periods of time, and every player scored.

> *A Basket, a Basket, a Basket boys,*
> *You Make the Baskets, We'll Make the Noise*
> *Yea Black, Yea White/Yea Team, Win tonight*

roared the chant as Waterloo rolled on its way through the second season.

Waterloo's initial momentum was, however, blunted. On December 22, in a game with Greenfield McClain in Highland County, a powerful Tiger team defeated them by two points, 26-24, in a sudden-death overtime. Thirteen-hundred fans jammed the McClain gym, an overflow crowd that often spilled onto the floor even as hundreds of others, unable to get tickets, gathered impatiently outside. After 56 wins, Waterloo had lost.

The loss to Greenfield left the Wonders neither discouraged nor dismayed. Green Township, Waverly, Ripley, and Portsmouth were turned back with ease as they closed out the year. The victory over Portsmouth was their third against schools in the Class A division. In early January they traveled to the Dayton Coliseum where they demolished Miamisburg, another Class A team, 43-12; two days later they headed east—stopping over in Chillicothe long enough for Hairston to trade his Chevrolet, its knee-action worn out, for a new Ford V-8 sedan—and clipped Marietta by 15 points.

Their weekly trips along the two-lane blacktops lined with telephone poles were punctuated by demonstrations of the Wonders' brash unorthodoxy. In late January, after a 7:00 p.m. home game tip-off against Chesapeake, they ran up a commanding halftime lead; leaving the reserves behind to finish the game, the starters hurried on to Jackson for their second game of the night. They beat Chesapeake 47-5 and Jackson 45-24.

These five young men played ball with an expertise that seemed innate. Their victories came easily, executed with the precision and aplomb of professionals, the rhythmic certainty of concert violinists or ballet dancers. They were, in unique combination, consummate basketball players and deliberate clowns. They mastered the range of conventional court tactics, and then moved beyond them to innovations that extended the limits of the game. Although the Wonders could execute the classic, two-hand set shot with grace, they preferred the color and accuracy of the more innovative lay-ups and hook shots. The full-court pass to the man at the top of the key, a dangerous play in the hands of novices, was a staple part of the Wonders' style. The

*The decaying Waterloo High School, circa 1995. Here the fabulous Waterloo Wonders delighted fans with a new style of basketball.*

Author's collection

behind-the-back pass of Wyman Roberts was swift and precise. The long, arched, set-shot of Orlyn Roberts from beyond mid-court was so accurate that it was a factor in his many scoring records. Their speed at handling, passing, and dribbling the ball riddled pressing defenses. When the Wonders were comfortably ahead or when they felt the urge, however, they continued to delight the fans with whimsies: two players starting a marble game in the center circle, or finishing a game with only one man on the floor. When a fan yelled "Shoot," the ball was passed into the crowd and a member of the audience was offered the honor. At other times one Wonder rolled the ball across the floor to a second who let it roll up his leg and into his hands. They often broke loose from a center jump and scored a basket for the opposition. When questioned by a sportswriter about their training regimen, the Wonder five and Coach Hairston, flaunting their inconformity, passed around a pack of Camels and lit up. But no such antics could conceal the fact that they were skilled and dedicated players.

During the early part of February, resplendent in new uniforms, Waterloo defeated five Class A teams in six days: Cincinnati St. Xavier, Gallipolis, and Chillicothe; Newport, Kentucky; and Huntington, West Virginia's Pony Express. The following week they easily defeated the tallest team in Kentucky, the famous Piner Giants from Kenton County, who averaged 6'5". They packed in crowds previously unknown in high school sports and, on 10-cent and 20-cent admissions, earned enough money to travel long distances, eat well, and stay in good hotels. They became celebrities wherever they went, tipping room-service bellboys, dressing as they pleased, and taking ingenuous delight in riding up and down hotel elevators. And on occasion, when the team had after-game snacks in Ironton, the coach, with team money, picked up the tab for the local admirers who crowded around them.

By mid-February, the team had become so celebrated that their appearances were feverishly promoted several days before the game.

An impending visit to Wilmington in Clinton County brought heavy press coverage. Individual players were profiled, and the legendary accomplishments of the team were reprised in the sports pages for several days. On game day a mob swirled outside the Wilmington College Gym hoping for seats. During the game many chilled fans waited at the doors for firsthand reports from the playing floor and afterward stayed to catch a glimpse of the players as they left the auditorium. The Wonders had proved they could conquer Class A teams, that their performance lived up to their reputation. They had become a competitive attraction for crowds. The traveling magic shows and the local movie theaters, where such features as Joan Blondell's *We're In the Money* played, were no longer the only entertainment in town.

The Wonders sailed through the remainder of the 1935 season. They traveled to Franklin in Warren County and, once again, along the white-lined road to Marietta, past the Burma-Shave signs: LISTEN BIRDS/THESE SIGNS COST MONEY/ SO ROOST AWHILE/ BUT DON'T GET FUNNY/ BURMA-SHAVE. One by one Waterloo's opponents fell: Wilmington, Highland, Nelsonville, and Green's Run.

The Wonders finished their regular season by defeating Chillicothe St. Mary's 42-18 and Canal Winchester 50-31. They had lost only three games.

In the Lawrence County tournament, they easily defeated Rome and Coal Grove, with 92 total points to the opposition's 23. In the sectional playoff held in Gallipolis, Waterloo began play against undefeated Racine, a team that some sports writers had picked to stop them. But when they went to the locker room the scoreboard read 48-18, Waterloo. In the Southeastern District tournament at Ohio University in Athens, they defeated Murray City 42-8, South Webster 48-24, and Sciotoville 36-22. For the second consecutive year, they had earned the right to represent Ohio's Class B schools at the fairgrounds coliseum. The Waterloo Wonders had three more games to play, three victories to gain to become only the second Ohio high

school basketball team in Class B to win consecutive state champion-
ships and to ensure themselves a place in basketball lore.

## GRADUATION AND BEYOND

Among the rituals of spring in rural communities, none is more
bittersweet than the local high school commencement. The joys of a
wedding and the sadness of a funeral are merged into one splendid
evening when coats and ties for the men, dressy frocks for the women,
and caps and gowns for the graduates are in order. At the Waterloo
High School commencement in 1935, Orlyn Roberts, Curtis
McMahon, and Stewart Wiseman walked the long march to the podium to receive their diplomas. Wyman Roberts and Beryl
Drummond sat in the audience and listened to the predictable re-
marks of the administrators and the memorized speeches delivered
in monotones by the honor students; they had not completed the
units necessary for a diploma. The Waterloo Wonders' high school
career was over.

Offers of athletic scholarships to Wonders players came from as
many as 50 colleges and universities across the United States. Adolph
Rupp, legendary coach of the University of Kentucky, attempted to
recruit the entire team. Early in the summer, Stewart Wiseman in-
formed fellow team members and his coach that he would leave for
college in the fall. The four remaining players, with Wiseman joining
in occasionally in the late spring of 1935, continued to play basketball as barnstormers, a vague status somewhere between amateur and
professional. At first they maintained their amateur status by agreeing to play only for expenses. Just a week after the state tournament,
they entered a Gold Medal basketball contest in New Boston. With
the help of two other local high school basketball favorites—George
Clark and Harold "Buddy" Kaiser—they left the weekend action with
the championship trophy.

Coach Hairston continued at Waterloo in 1935 - 36, and he also
provided management for the Wonders' barnstorming tours. Games

were scheduled against local high school teams and with industrial league fives. For these games they received, after expenses, payments ranging from $25 to $50 per player with the coach receiving a share.

In the 1930s distinctions between amateur sports, barnstorming, and professional ball were ill-defined, and many situations arose that were beyond the scope of official sanctions. A series of unpleasant events marked the Wonders' transition from amateurs to semiprofessionals: certain members of the Waterloo Board of Education, after raising questions about the lack of accountability for the team's earnings, denied the Wonders an opportunity to attend the banquet given by the Ironton Chamber of Commerce that was to precede a game between Waterloo and the Oldsmobile Specials; complaints were made about the reserved admission price of 60 cents for an Ironton-Waterloo contest; and Dr. J. D. Swango, president of the Waterloo school board, threatened to resign and move to Kentucky after an unpleasant altercation with two of the Waterloo players near his office. The Waterloo community, once solidly behind the Wonders, became an imbroglio of dissension and support as word of the financial controversy circulated in the spring of 1936. And in that spring, Magellan Hairston resigned as coach and principal and returned to farming. In 1938 he returned to his coaching position at Waterloo in a more favorable political climate. And in 1941 Hairston's team again went to the first round of the Class B tournament, where they were defeated.

In the fall of 1936, Stewart Wiseman went off to college, and the remaining four Wonders accepted jobs with the Frigidaire Corporation in Dayton and joined the company's industrial league team. A highlight of the Wonders' professional careers was a series with the New York Celtics, the best basketball team in the nation. They had first played the Celtics the year before in Ironton. Against a lineup that included three of professional basketball's most famous players— Nat Hickey, Davey Banks, and Joe Lapchick—they lost the game but played with such intensity that a rematch was inevitable. They recruited a former Ohio State star, Bill Hoskett, Sr., a 6'3" pivotman, to play the open position in their second game against the Celtics. The game was held in Lima, before a capacity crowd, and this time the Wonders came within one point of defeating the nation's leading professionals. Interest in the Wonders-Celtics encounters became a statewide phenomena, and by 1937 the third game was arranged and booked into Cleveland's Public Hall. And before 7,000 screaming fans in the giant arena, with Orlyn Roberts scoring a game-high 18 points, the Wonders accomplished their goal—they defeated the Celtics 47-39.

The Wonders had established themselves on the professional tour. They, along with the Celtics, the Harlem Renaissance, the Philadelphia Spahs, and the House of David, took their place among the great teams of the era. They continued to compete until the early 1940s when World War II disrupted the nation's social order. Hairston, who had resumed the coaching duties at Waterloo in 1938, left the school and the profession for good in 1943. Orlyn Roberts played on the Camp Lee, Virginia, army team that occasionally played in Madison Square Garden. Both he and Wyman Roberts played in several professional games after the war. Beryl Drummond continued to play semi-professional ball, with such teams as the Acme Aviators, the Wright Field Kitty-Hawks, White Motors, the Toledo Mercurys, Sucher Victory Meats, and the Toledo Jeeps. He participated in tournaments for several years at the Chicago International Amphitheater (with the Dayton Bombers) and at the Chicago Stadium (with the Toledo Jeeps and Acme Aviators). Drummond's career included games with or against the basketball greats of his era, including Zach Clayton, Reece "Goose" Tatum, Nat "Sweetwater" Clifton, Eyre "Bruiser" Satch, Charles "Tarzan" Cooper, Dutch Dehnert, and Bill "Wee Willie" Smith. Drummond played his last game in the winter of 1952, when, after a disappointing game at the Knights of Columbus Gym, in Columbus, he retired. Eight years later, in 1960, the team name, Waterloo Wonders, and the high school disappeared, when Waterloo High was consolidated with the Windsor High School into the Symmes Valley School District.

Magellan Harriston died in 1968 at 61 and is buried in Ironton, Woodland Cemetery; Orlyn Roberts died in 1983 at 67; Wyman Roberts died in 1985 at 72; Beryl Drummond died in 1983 at 65; they are buried in Flagg Springs cemetery in Lawrence County, Ohio; Stewart Wiseman died in 1996 at 79 and is buried in Athens, Ohio.

*Bronze plaque from the Ohio Historical Society memorializes the Waterloo Wonders basketball team, Ohio State Route 141, Waterloo, Ohio.*

*The driver of this peddling wagon is deciding the worth of a farm product offered in trade for an item from the city. Left, Nancy Goodall, far right, Robert Goodall, standing on Jenkins Road in Gallia County, Ohio, near Waterloo. Later, old school buses were converted into peddling wagons.*

# Dog Days

In the dog days of August, I sat inside the living room on the web springs of an old army cot. World War I surplus my father bought about 1920. I had come down from Columbus, Ohio, to have one last look at the old home place on Williams Creek. Busy with my job up north and my own family, I had not made the three-hour trip south toward the Ohio River since my mother died over a year ago. My wife and I had talked many times about buying my brother's share in the house, fixing it up, maybe getting a pony for the kids, and coming back on summer weekends. Today, the heat was oppressive. Ladybugs crawled up and down the dirty wallpaper. Empty wine bottles, old newspapers, and coal ashes were scattered around on the worn linoleum floor covering. Outside, by the porch where my mother used to pick red roses from the trellis to decorate graves in May, a horseweed grew strong and proud.

I got to thinking about what it was like here when I was little. I was born in this house as were my brothers and sisters, all older. One brother, born five years before me, died with the flu. My oldest brother, George, born in 1920, remembered the undertaker standing in the kitchen selling a tiny coffin guaranteed to be waterproof. Yes, he would be glad to wait for his money until the tobacco crop was sold in December, Christmas time, 1930. My dad, a few hired hands who came and went, and my brother, milked a few cows, tied tobacco, cleaned out the cow barn, carried in coal, and hauled out ashes as the winter passed. In the summers they chopped ragweeds with a goose-neck hoe and suckered tobacco until their hands were black with gum. They pulled big, juicy worms off the leaves and slammed them against hard clods of dirt. One of the hired hands would bite their heads off and spit them out. Anyway, he didn't swallow them. But Momma, she was a caution. Inside the house cooking, cleaning, reading the paper, struggling to get through the Bible one more time. She would set up her quilting frames and sew the day away working with scraps of old clothes. She made her dresses and other articles of clothing from old feed sacks that, thoughtfully, the manufacturer had added col-

*Appalachian family with Ohio River fish, circa 1940.*

Tina Bryan collection

orful prints to the otherwise plain cloth. She picked wild blackberries and raspberries and strained the juice out of a dish cloth to make jelly.

One of my uncles used to bring my grandfather, William, to visit. Gangrene had taken one of his legs. He walked on crutches. His right pants leg was always folded above the knee, held up with large safety pins. When he died, I stood to the side and watched a group of men bring his coffin into his house through a window. Friends and family sat up all night near his body in the eerie glow of coal-oil lamps. On the day of the funeral they sang his favorite hymn, *Life Is Like A Mountain Railroad*, before six pallbearers loaded his coffin into a black Cadillac hearse. I don't remember feeling sad. But I knew something important had happened.

When I went to college, I learned about tribes of people from alien lands, brown people who were called "hunters and gatherers." My family might not have been nomads, but food and goods were taken from the land. And the land did not give them up easy. My Mamma would go into the fields in early spring with a butcher knife and a dishpan in search of greens. She took the hickory nuts, walnuts, hazelnuts, butternuts, and chestnuts we gathered in the fall, shelled them and baked them in cakes and cookies. She would send us across the rill and into the woods to gather peaches, pears, grapes, raspberries, blackberries, gooseberries, apples, and persimmons, whatever was in season growing wild. These fruits were eaten raw, made into jams and jellies, or served with thick cream and sugar as desserts. My Dad used steel traps to capture minks, muskrats, and beavers from Indian Guyan Creek. These pelts were sold or traded for goods. He took squirrels, rabbits, raccoons, ruffed grouse, wild ducks, deer, and turkeys with a twenty-gauge shotgun. Dad dressed the game and we ate it. As Momma used to say, "Eat that before it eats you." The creek gave up catfish, suckers, bass, sunfish, frogs, and soft-shell turtles. A common way to catch fish was to seine them with a piece of screen wire at riffles in the creek. I saw my dad pull turtles out of the underwater holes in the muddy banks by their tails. He would put them in a coffee sack, fling it over his back, and carry them home. Our grandpa told us that if a turtle bit you it would not let go until it thundered. He said if you left a horsehair in warm creek water, it would turn into a snake. When I found out these things were not true, I was sad. Cleaning fish and dressing game were primitive activities; but when cooked the results were good. Like a French cook can make a snail delicious. Picking berries was slow, sweaty work. As the sun bore down, we carried gallon buckets through briars and bushes, between rocks where copperhead snakes lay in wait, and as the long morning passed, one berry at a time, and filled them with wild berries. Enough for a few jars of jelly and jam. Sometimes you could sell a few good quarts for a dime apiece. Dad set traps for wild game in the cold winter on frozen creek banks. If someone found the precious mink before you did, it would be stolen. And, sometimes, wandering dogs would get caught in the jaws of steel traps which could mean trouble with a neighbor.

Domestic animals were a part of living. We milked 12 cows by hand twice each day, 365 days a year. In the summer, we cooled the milk by pouring it into a cooler filled with water taken from the well. In winter when the ground wasn't frozen, cattle tramped through mud and cow manure on their way to and from the cow barn. As peasant farmers who couldn't afford a bull, when a cow was in heat, we walked her to a neighbor's house to get her bred. This was a violent act. A two-ton bull would snort heavy breaths into the winter air, brace its rear legs against the barn floor and shove the cow's head against the wall with severe thrusts. Just another puzzling scene for a child. We slopped hogs through spring and summer, butchered in the fall. I stood there shivering in the cold while my father put a twenty-two caliber bullet through the hog's head. Dad hooked a chain from a tree limb to the hog's hind legs. After the hog was hoisted up, a man would slash the scalded animal's stomach and empty the stinking guts into buckets.

*Log barn with sheds from the 19th century.*

Author's collection

My Momma, she hated snakes. A big black snake crawled up in the yard one day looking for shade. I ran into the house. Momma grabbed a hoe and chopped its head off. She'd sling that hoe and grunt every time it hit the snake. When it stopped moving, she got a big piece of it, threw it over the clothesline, said it would make it rain. It did, too. Then she'd give me a hot biscuit, send me out to play and say, "Don't let that durn rooster take it away from you."

Once I saw a cow lying on her side in the pasture trying to give birth. My father and a hired hand tied a rope around the calf's neck and pulled it out. Sick cows and horses had to be drenched. One man would hold the horse's head sideways while the other stuck an old wine bottle full of medicine in her mouth, letting the liquid go down in giant gulps. When a large animal died, dad sold it for a few dollars to some guy who loaded it on a truck and hauled it away.

I was taken to church as soon as I was old enough to leave the house. Preachers went into long chants switching from Bible quotes to their own exhortations. Great efforts were made to get everyone past the age of twelve saved. No one was spared from this process. Those people who hadn't confessed their sins at the altar, accepted Christ as their savior, and stopped cussing, drinking, and stealing were destined for an eternal hell. Everything was black and white. No middle ground. Saved or sinner. The choice was yours. Two pictures from these times stay in my head. The classic, bearded Jesus looking toward heaven and, above the battery-powered Philco radio where the fireside chats came in, Franklin D. Roosevelt. Both saviors. Hearing intense sermons, singing the mournful hymns, attending baptisms in the creek left an indelible mark on anyone who grew up here. Through age, experience, and education, you might see things different. But there were times when these sights, sounds, and smells would creep back into your head.

The house we lived in was Midwest vernacular. Tin roof with a weather vane and lightning rods. No insulation. In the winter, Mamma melted salve in a tablespoon held over the heat that rose from the chimney of a coal-oil lamp, rubbed it on our chests, and tucked us under three or four heavy, homemade quilts and comforters. The fire in the open fireplace that flickered scary shadows about the room was banked with ashes for the night. By morning, our bedrooms were about the same temperature as the outside. In summer, the dog days of August brought dry weather and stifling heat. My brother and I lay in bed with the windows and doors open until the heat broke with long cadences of thunder bursts and lightning flashing in the sky. Great torrents of rain pounded the tin roof. Scared, we climbed out of our beds and rushed to get in with our parents.

I've heard people suggest that seeing animals exercise their libidos gave humans insight into their own manners of marrying and having babies. Momma told me that when a cow had a calf, she had found it. Same way with kittens. I didn't associate this with human behavior. Still don't. Most of the men I knew didn't talk dirty in front of women. Momma called that blackguarding. We saved that pleasure for the barn where the men ran everything. The same words we were told not to say back then are the same ones we tell our children not to say now. In that respect, we haven't advanced. My family and others I knew well were modest people. Naked bodies were never seen by others. In fact, many never saw their own bodies. The men I knew wore long pants and long sleeve shirts the year around. My dad wore long underwear in the summer, a lighter version of long johns. The women wore dresses that reached below the knees. We seldom took baths, wishing to avoid the hassle of bathing from a wash pan and a cloth in the kitchen. But when we did take a bath, it was a crude one. We were told to, "Wash up as far as possible, down as far as possible. Once in awhile, wash possible."

I got up, finally, and walked through the house. Up a steep stairway to the attic which served as a bedroom. The mud dauber nests were still there and the dead new wasp nests were empty now. I went through the two downstairs bedrooms where the peeling wallpaper with its once bright floral prints faded. The kitchen, dining room, and living room comprised the rest of the house, looking smaller now than I remembered. I walked outside to the barn, dilapidated now

*Samantha McDonald, circa 1935. Rural Appalachian women dressed for modesty, the sun, and hard work.*

but not that much different than before. Tier poles, leaning frame, parts of the tin roof gone. The creek nearby, the rock houses, the branch that ran down from the hollow were as I remembered them, rough, as natural as they had been for a million years, except for the moss covered etchings of initials my older brothers had carved into the stone years past.

As the shadows outside got longer, I thought there was no way making this place a weekend retreat and hanging onto the reverie. Columbus was three hours away. The kids were more interested in spending Saturdays at the Great Northern Shopping Center or Penney's Outlet, anyway. We couldn't leave the place vacant as one might have done before. Too many weed growers and food stamp addicts had squatted on coal company land just up the road. The old place would pass to new times. Maybe we could sell it to someone and let them strip the coal. Who would care if the rill that runs by the house turned yellow with sulphur? Leave this land of sea grass that bends in the winds of April and the stark song of the rain crow to the shifting movements of men and nature.

# Murder on Greasy Ridge

*They loved, but the story we cannot unfold,*
*They scorned, but the heart of the haughty is cold;*
*They grieved, but no wail from their slumbers will come;*
*They joyed, but the tongue of their gladness is dumb.*
—William Knox

The tobacco in the flats along Greasy Ridge was tall and golden brown. The corn silks that hung down from the ears of corn were black and the crop was ready to be cut. The milk cows were fat, and the cream they provided was rich and thick. The raspberries and black-berries that grew wild along the banks of Buckeye Creek had been picked and canned for winter. The air was filled with the musky smells of early fall. This was the summer of 1935 on Greasy Ridge, late August. The family of Eli Roy Massie looked forward to October and a respite from the long summer dog days.

Massie, his wife Mary, and the youngest of their four children, Faith Ilene, lived on a 260 acre farm just down the road from the Greasy Ridge Post Office. Faith, a 31-year-old divorced school teacher, and her mother managed the farm and kept house in a two-story colonial style home that was among the best on the ridge. They also looked after Roy Massie who was dying of bone cancer.

Faith was born in the old house in 1904 and went to nearby Tagg Grade School until she completed the eighth grade. At age 14 she had already begun to show her family and friends that she was not a typi-cal farm girl from Greasy Ridge. Her interest in the arts, in books, in piano, and in academic achievement was different from most other rural teenagers. Tradition was for local girls to quit school, learn to make beds, marry a local boy from a good family, and have a house full of babies.

Faith was a shy young girl in gingham dresses and patent leather shoes with buckled straps across pink socks. She and her family were known all along Greasy Ridge Road, which begins near the Ohio River at Bradrick, a small village in eastern Lawrence County where the ferry boat across the river to Huntington, West Virginia, once ran. Greasy Ridge runs north from Bradrick and snakes along the top of the hill until it drops down into Lecta, 22 miles north. A county road, it passes through the once robust little post office and grocery stops of Dobbstown, Rappsburg, and Greasy Ridge. The road got its name, old timers say, from the sharp slope of the hills on both sides that caused grazing cows to fall and slide into Buckeye Creek.

Faith often traveled with her father to Dobbstown, where Dr. Irvin Mayberry saw patients in his home office for a buck-and-a-half. For two, he would pull his Chrysler out and make a house call. Near Mayberry's office, Dunfee's grocery did a big business selling groceries, notions, hardware, feed, and, of special interest to Faith, red and green pieces of penny candy displayed in large glass jars. A few miles west toward Ironton, at Willow Wood, Walter Higgins sold new Chevrolets to the few who could afford them.

Six miles north of Dobbstown was Rappsburg, located at a crossroads where travelers from Gallia, Vinton, and Jackson Counties passed on their way to Ironton and other points west. Owen Callicoat sold gas and groceries. Oscar Moore owned a barn where pinhookers bid on tobacco and shipped it away to markets in Maysville, Kentucky, and Cincinnati.

Farther north, four miles from Rappsburg, was the combination grocery school and Greasy Ridge Post Office, the Old Baptist Church which was founded in 1807, and the Lecta Eagles Club picnic ground, where the popular July 4th celebration was held each year. And just over the hill was Waterloo High School, home of the legendary Wa-

Author's collection

*Long since gone broke, this store on Greasy Ridge was owned by Wilbur Dunfee.*

terloo Wonders basketball team who won the state basketball tournaments for Class B schools in 1934 and 1935.

Faith Massie's venture into the larger world began in the fall of 1921 when she went 25 miles south to enroll for her final two years at Ironton High School in the Lawrence County seat. She boarded with a family and walked to school. Her high school records show that she was a B or better student. The caption beside her yearbook picture listed her nickname as "Toots," and "Youth I do adore thee," as her favorite saying.

Faith Massie, an attractive and respected girl in the community, returned home to spend the summer of 1923 with her family. In the fall, she enrolled at Rio Grande College in Gallia County and studied elementary education. After two years there, she returned again to Greasy Ridge, obtained a teaching certificate, and taught at Tagg Grade School near Rappsburg.

While she continued to teach at Tagg, she courted and married a

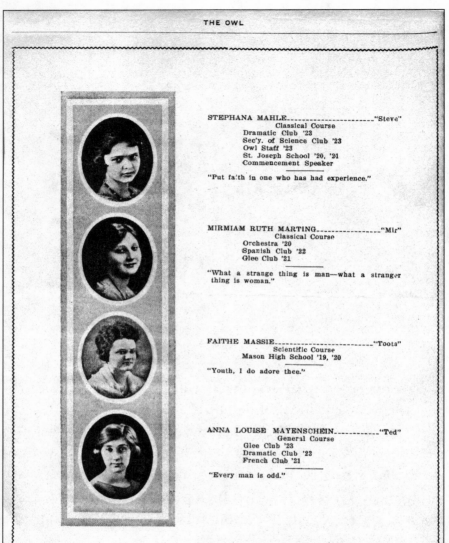

THE OWL

STEPHANA MAHLE............................"Steve"
Classical Course
Dramatic Club '23
Sec'y. of Science Club '23
Owl Staff '23
St. Joseph School '20, '21
Commencement Speaker

"Put faith in one who has had experience."

MIRMIAM RUTH MARTING..................."Mir"
Classical Course
Orchestra '20
Spanish Club '22
Glee Club '21

"What a strange thing is man—what a stranger thing is woman."

FAITHE MASSIE.............................."Toots"
Scientific Course
Mason High School '19, '20

"Youth, I do adore thee."

ANNA LOUISE MAYENSCHEIN............."Ted"
General Course
Glee Club '23
Dramatic Club '23
French Club '21

"Every man is odd."

Author's collection

*Faith Massie, Ironton, Ohio, High School Year Book, 1923.*

man from the village of Aid named Roy Shiverly, a union that was short and unhappy. After the divorce, she continued her education and transferred the credits earned at Rio Grande to Ohio University in Athens, where, on June 3, 1935, she was awarded a Bachelor of Science degree in education with a major in economics. The divorce, rather than having a negative effect on her future, had stimulated

Faith to achieve something that few on Greasy Ridge had accomplished, a college degree from a major university.

While Faith was at Ohio University, she spent many weekends visiting at the home of her friend, Alice Mossbarger, in Columbus. It was on one of these visits that she was introduced to a 42-year-old widower, Charles Horton, who was the father of two children. The two of them got on well together in spite of their different cultural backgrounds. Charles worked as a freight agent for the Norfolk and Western Railroad, a good job in the 1930s when many qualified men had no jobs at all. After their first meeting, they continued to see each other periodically on weekends at the Massie farm. Breaking from local tradition, Horton was a welcome houseguest at the Massie's.

Charles Horton grew up on Third Street in Columbus and attended public school there. Even as he hung out at the bustling corner of Broad and High streets, Faith Massie picked blackberries and milked the family cow on Greasy Ridge. Columbus was only 120 miles north but the culture, ethos, and its 300,000 residents comprised a land that was alien to most rural people.

On a typical summer afternoon in downtown Columbus, the LeVeque Tower cast its long shadow east along Broad Street. Businessmen, lawyers and politicians lounged in their Palm Beach suits, drinking martinis in the Sapphire Room of the Deshler-Wallick Hotel at Broad and High. Around the corner on West Broad, the Lowes Broad theater showed films like Laurel and Hardy in *Bonnie Scotland* and provided an air-conditioned respite. The light bulbs on the three-story tall sign at Roy's Jewelers, on the northeast corner of Broad and High, blinked with little effect against the bright sunlight. Through the summers of the 1920s, while Faith Massie walked behind her dad as he plowed with a horse-drawn cultivator, Charles Horton spent his idle hours in the pool rooms and ice cream shops in downtown Columbus.

On the Saturday of August 24, 1935, Faith Massie arose early, got dressed, had breakfast with her mother and father, and prepared to

*House of Roy Massie, Faith's father, Greasy Ridge.*

drive to Ironton. She spent some extra minutes with her father, Roy. Shortly after 8 a.m., two hours after sunrise, she backed her father's 1934 Dodge roadster out of the driveway, shifted into low gear, and headed toward the village of Aid and turned left on state Route 141 to Ironton. Both car windows were down and the windshield was cranked open to bring air into the car. Although it was still early morning, the dry August heat that would last all week was already hanging close to the ground.

As she drove toward Ironton and the railway depot on Second Street, she thought about the new school year at Windsor High School, where she was set to begin teaching after Labor Day. She thought of her father who was sick, perhaps near death. Money she owed her brother Everett to attend college was also on her mind. But the main thing in Faith Massie's head was her relationship with Charles Horton. Horton always traveled from Columbus to Ironton by train because, as an employee of the railroad, he had an honorary pass. Faith was expecting him on the 10 a.m. train this particular Saturday morning.

Faith Massie was confident that she could discuss her problems and feelings with Charles. He was a mature gentleman who had always been respectful of her feelings and wishes. Perhaps influenced by his quiet nature, Faith perceived him as a patient and intelligent person. Horton's nature was pleasant and mannerly. His sense of humor was urbane. His prematurely gray hair and his affectation toward linen jackets and silk shirts only added to the mystique of Charles Horton.

The train from Columbus was on time. Faith helped him load his small suitcase into the trunk, and within a few minutes she and Horton were speeding north on Route 141 heading back to the Massie farm. They made small talk about the week's past events and the heat.

They arrived at the farm in time for dinner with the Massie family. They relaxed through the afternoon and, after supper, went outside to play tennis and wander around the yard, the garden, and the barnyard where the chickens ran loose. Later, Horton lounged in the house with the family, listening to the battery-powered, Zenith console radio, and Faith worked on a tapestry she was doing before all retired early for bed. The family and guest slept late on Sunday morning. It

*Little Indian Guyan Creek near Scottown, Ohio. Locals spell it "Polkadotte" Creek, and pronounce it "Pokiedot."*

Vicki Wilson collection

was the 25th of August, and there was only one long summer week-end left, Labor Day, before the local schools were set to open and Faith would have to return to work. In addition to the Massie family and Horton, their dinner guests that Sunday included Faith's older brother Bernard, his wife Della White Massie, and their 10-year-old daughter Maridell. Lois White, Maridell's 8-year-old cousin who lived three miles away, was also among the guests.

The Massie family and their guests enjoyed a traditional country dinner of southern fried chicken, green beans, mashed potatoes with gravy, ham and watermelon. For dessert, they had homemade ice cream which had been made that morning in a hand-cranked ice cream freezer.

After the leisurely meal, Faith and Charles did the dishes while the older folks lay around. The children played outside. About 3 p.m., Faith and Charles went for a walk out the ridge to the tobacco barn. Faith wanted to weigh herself on the produce scales there. They told everyone they would be back soon.

An hour later, Charles Horton returned to the house and said that Faith wanted her glasses. He went upstairs and within a few minutes came back down into the living room. As he walked through the room one of the family members noticed that he was holding his left hand over the left outside pocket of his summer sport coat. As time for supper approached, about 5 p.m., Bernard Massie and his wife sent the two girls, Maridell and Lois, to the tobacco barn to tell Faith and Charles that they were going back to Ironton. They wanted to tell them good-bye before leaving. The girls were cautioned to be on the lookout for deadly copperhead snakes.

Lois and Maridell walked and skipped merrily out the road toward the tobacco barn, more than pleased to go about their task. The girls pulled themselves easily up into the section of the barn that was floored. Their first sight was one that would stay with them forever. The lifeless bodies of Faith Massie and Charles Horton were stretched across the produce scales. Faith was lying face down in a pool of blood.

Charles was lying on his back. Between them on the floor was a .38-caliber blue steel, long barrel Colt automatic pistol. A short-handled, blood-stained ore pick was also lying at the scene.

Maridell and Lois ran toward the house in shock. Maridell screamed, "Grandma, Grandma, Aunt Faith's dead! Aunt Faith's dead!" Faith's mother, Mary, was in the barnyard near the house gathering eggs. She could tell that the children were scared, that they were not playing tricks. Maridell then went into the house to tell her father, Bernard. He was preparing to give Roy Massie a shot of morphine and, at first, he told Maridell to stop bothering him with tomfoolery.

Mary Massie, after viewing the dead bodies in horror went back to the house and got a bedsheet which she took to the barn and placed over the bodies. She returned to the house and called Lois White's grandfather, James, on the telephone. Lawrence County Sheriff Bernard Monte was called and within an hour, the dirt road was lined with cars which belonged to neighbors, law enforcement officials and the Phillips Funeral Home of Waterloo.

Deputy Sheriff H.M. Shattuck and coroner W.W. Lynd investigated the incident at the site. Faith had been struck five times in the head with the sharp end of a pick which Roy Massie had used to dig coal from a small coal bank located on the farm. The blade of the pick was matted with blood and hair. The officers also found that a bullet had passed through Faith's head from left to right just below the ears. There was no blood from this wound, and it appeared she was dead when the shot was fired. Charles Horton was lying on his back with wounds indicating that a bullet had entered the right side of his head, two inches above the ear and emerged on the left side, three inches above the ear. Blood trickled from his mouth. His eyes, still open, stared blankly at the tobacco tier poles overhead. The barn scales rested at 117 pounds, Faith's weight. A romance that had begun on a gay note in Columbus where the sound of jazz music drifted across a summer room was over. There amidst mud dauber nests, blood, dust and oppressive heat in a dirty tobacco barn Faith and Charles lay dead. The next day, newspaper boys in Columbus hawked the evening *Dispatch* at the state fair shouting "Columbus man crushes girl's head on Greasy Ridge: Read all about it!" Coroner Lynd pronounced the event, on the basis of evidence and speculation, a murder-suicide. Faith Massie's body was prepared for burial on Greasy Ridge; Horton's corpse was held at the Phillips Funeral Home until it was claimed by his older daughter in Columbus.

A motive for this bizarre act emerged from interviews with the family and friends. Faith Massie had been dating Charles Horton for more than a year and letters from her to him, found in his luggage after the murder, contained messages of love. Speculation about the motive centered around the belief she had either reneged on a commitment to marriage or was asking that he back off for awhile. It may have been that her decision to take a teaching job at Windsor High School rather than move to Columbus angered Horton. He may not have been sympathetic to Faith's need to stay with her family and help care for her ill father. Perhaps she rejected him for personal reasons and gave other excuses in an attempt to avoid confrontation.

Charles Horton was, possibly, a psychopathic killer in a linen sport coat and brown-and-white wing tip shoes. He was carrying a handgun, but this was not unusual for a railway traveler in the 1930s. The fact that he mortally wounded Faith with a mattock, before the gun was brought out, leads to the belief that it was not murder in the first degree. For reasons which are forever lost to separate tombs in the counties of Lawrence and Franklin, Charles Horton killed in a fit of short-lived rage. But within minutes after the first attack, he calmly walked back to the house, picked up a gun, made sure Faith was dead, then killed himself.

By noon on Wednesday, August 28, hundreds of cars lined both sides of the road for a mile in each direction from the Old Baptist Church on Greasy Ridge. The cars, parked among the milk weeds off the edge of the road after the small church parking lot was filled, barely left room for passage along the dusty, gravel road. Right after high

Doris Gettys collection

*Old Baptist Church, Greasy Ridge.*

noon, the black, shiny Cadillac hearse of the Phillips Funeral Home crunched through the gravel in front of the church. Mr. Phillips swung open the rear door of the hearse and pulled out the silver gray metal coffin. Six men grasped the long handles on the coffin and gently carried it up the church steps, through the door, and placed it on a collapsible catafalque. The pallbearers rolled the coffin to the front of the church, past the rows of mourners, and the undertaker carefully opened it. Reverend Jerry Bruce read Faith's obituary. A quartet sang a capella,

> *When I've gone the last mile of the way*
> *I will rest at the close of the day*
> *And I know there are joys that await me*
> *When I've gone the last mile of the way.*

After a message of comfort to the family and friends about Faith, and the need for those listening who were not prepared for death to repent, the service was again turned over to the undertaker.

Mr. Phillips gave a cue to the people seated and, one row at a time, the mourners filed slowly past the body of Faith Massie. The undertaker then stepped to the back of the church and motioned for those who could not get into the small church to come forward and pay their last respects. After the ritual of friends and neighbors viewing the body, the family was signaled to approach the coffin. They stood there in tears as the veil over the body was lifted. They took this death hard. The fairest in the family and on the ridge lay in endless sleep. Finally, Mr. Phillips moved forward and, as the family returned to their pews, gently rolled the stuffed satin lining of the coffin inside the half lid and closed it. He took a small metal rod from his pocket, inserted it into a latch mechanism and twisted it tightly closed, forever.

At 2:00 p.m., Faith's body was carried from the church to a spot on the northwest side of the cemetery adjacent to the church and placed on a platform above the open grave. The mounds of red clay and sandstone soil which had been removed from the grave were covered with a blanket of artificial grass. Brief graveside rites were performed, and

*Faith Massie's grave, Old Baptist Church graveyard, Greasy Ridge. There may be a place bleaker than this on a winter evening, but the author has never seen it.*

Author's collection

Faith Massie, age 31, was buried in the family graveyard. By evening, the flowers that had been placed on the grave were wilted, the crushed grass had sprung back, and the cigarette butts left by grave diggers lay about the area. Greasy Ridge was silent except for the sounds of the killdeer.

The preceding day in Columbus, 13 blocks south of Broad and High Streets, at the A.K. Graumlich Funeral Home (the establishment that had provided local help in bringing Abraham Lincoln's body to and from the state capitol building in April 1865), funeral services for Charles Horton, now in repose, were in progress. A baroque lamp stood at the head of the coffin casting a subdued, rose-colored glow around the area near the catafalque. Horton's family and a small group of his friends and associates sat near the front of the air-cooled room. Recorded organ music came from the speakers on the wall, soothing the mourners with the background music to the hymn, *Near the Cross.*

After the brief service, the coffin containing Charles Horton's body was wheeled outside to the curb and placed inside a 1932 Studebaker hearse. The family and close friends walked slowly behind. As the hearse was being loaded, the family entered the backseat of a Packard limousine. The other mourners hurried on to their private cars. A police car, lights blinking, led the hearse and the funeral procession north on High Street to North Broadway, West to the Olentangy River Road and through the gates of Union Cemetery. There, under a canvas tent, a preacher led prayers amidst a vast, flat acreage containing hundreds of large monuments and mausoleums. Within 100 yards of the busy thoroughfare of the Olentangy River Road, Charles Horton's body was buried beside the grave of his wife. The graves are unmarked.

# Elijah's Funeral

The tombstones in the graveyard on the Good Hope knoll stood dark and strong against the February winds. Twisted brown strands of summer's growth of sweet clover were woven against the red dirt. Elegant oak trees with black trunks, great limbs, and deserted birds' nests cast silhouettes against the haze hanging above the Ohio River. The deep, lingering sounds of the bell on the white, batten church across the road drifted over the ridges and settled among the distant rills like fog. Two men in gum boots worked at an open grave bailing out the water that had seeped in overnight. Finishing their work, they sat on the fake grass that covered the mound of dirt taking deep drags on roll-your-own Buglers. Elijah Bennet, the owner of 700 acres of hill and bottom land, boss of a dozen sharecroppers, was dead. A neigh-

*Preacher's stand, common in east Virginia. Funerals and prayer meetings were held outdoors when the weather was good.*

bor had found him slumped over the wheel of his Cadillac two days ago and, after two nights of family and friends sitting up in the home with his body, preaching and burial were forthcoming.

Fords and Chevvies with rusted running boards, a Willys Overland, and a few horse-drawn expresses were parked at the edge of the grove by the church. Two young women in long dresses, looking down, hurried up the path from the outside toilet and entered the church. A black Packard hearse, fresh gobs of mud dripping from its fender wells and tires, spewed exhaust fumes into the damp air as it pulled in front of the church door. A dozen men in wool Mackinaws and overall jackets stood off to the side. No one spoke.

The undertaker and the preacher, splendid in dark suits and black wingtips, stepped out of the hearse and walked to the back. The preacher watched as the undertaker swung the back door open, unlatched the coffin, and let it slide slowly toward him. Six men in frayed wool suits grasped the handles that ran along the mahogany coffin and carried it to the church door, up the concrete steps, placed it on a rolling catafalque and rolled it to the front of the church. The undertaker, moving with grace and authority, opened the half-lid, gently arranging the white satin surrounding Bennet's body. Family members, seated on the reserved front rows, broke down with heavy sobs and stark grief as the corpse, laid out in blue serge and red tie, lay in repose. The room was redolent of sweet flowers and powder patted onto the veiled faces of Bennet's widow, three daughters, and other Christian women of the church. A pristine young girl struck a gentle minor chord on the upright piano above the altar and rolled her hands into treble riffs softened by a muted foot pedal. The Athalia quartet stepped forward, opened hymnals, sounded a pitch, and sang:

> *When I've gone the last mile of the way*
> *I will rest at the close of the day*
> *And I know there are joys that await me*
> *When I've gone the last mile of the way*

The church superintendent, a gnarled old man in a vest and suspenders, stepped forward and read from the Bible:

> *But the heavens and the earth, which are now, by the*
> *Same word are kept in store, reserved unto fire against the*
> *Day of judgment and perdition of ungodly men. The*
> *Lord is not slack concerning his promise, as some men*
> *Count slackness; but is longsuffering to usward, not*
> *Willing that any should perish, but that all should come*
> *To repentance*

Preacher Bill Lunsford stood behind the pulpit in the glow of peach-colored electric lights that stood at each end of the coffin. Flames whipped inside the pot-bellied stove that gave off heat near the amen corner. Bennet's family continued to cry as Lunsford spoke, saying, "Folks, you know when a good man like Elijah Bennet goes home, it just strengthens our faith in the good Lord. Oh, what a merciful God he is. Elijah came to the Lord many years ago when he was a young man of 17. He was baptized that summer in Indian Guyan Creek. He never faltered in his faith. Like Paul, he fought a good fight, he kept the faith, and now he has finished his course. Why many's the time I have stopped at Elijah's place, maybe he'd be telling his hired hands which field to plow, or what time to bring the cows in to milk. We'd sit there in the shade and talk for hours. He was always proud of his family and his church. We'd talk about how he loved the Lord and how his faith had made it possible for him and his wife, Grace, to survive the death of two tiny babies in the flu epidemic of 1918. You know the doctors couldn't do much back then. All these graveyards are full of children, some buried back on the hills in family plots fenced off to keep cattle from turning over the monuments. When a neighbor was sick or needed help, he could count on Elijah Bennet." Lunsford went on for nearly an hour, his voice rising then falling to a whisper. He ended his sermon telling the congregation that those who were saved would surely see their dead loved ones in the great beyond and those who had not accepted Christ would spend eternity in a burning hell that went on forever.

Again, the quartet sang:

> *Farther along we'll know all about it*
> *Farther along we'll understand why*
> *Cheer up, my brother, live in the sunshine*
> *We'll understand it all by and by*

The undertaker moved forward. He walked down the aisle, leaned out the church door, and motioned for those who chose to see Elijah's body to step inside and pass by the coffin. A dozen or more men and boys, hats held in their hands against bibbed overalls, walked slowly by letting their eyes sweep down Elijah's face before they moved back to the casual setting outside. Those who sat in the back pews continued the ritual, and row-by-row moved up and down the aisles amidst the sounds of creaking pews, crying babies, and corduroy pants legs brushing together.

The undertaker led the family forward to stand in front of the coffin. The widow and children wailed in grief as others looked on. The 10 minutes they stood there were long. Long like the winter drabness that comes down in the Appalachian plateau. Long like the endless grief that overshadows joy. Finally, the undertaker led the family to their seats. He turned and leaned over the coffin, his large body blocking the view. Gold cufflinks in his white shirt flashing, he worked his seasoned hands in a slow rhythm pushing the satin over on the body. He pushed up the side panels, unleashed the brace that held the lid open, took a metal rod from his pocket, inserted it into the coffin lock and twisted it shut. Elijah Bennet was committed to darkness for all time.

The pallbearers picked up the coffin at the church door and carried it through the graveyard to the open grave. The family and close friends walked behind in a slow, mournful gait along the gravel path, across the dead growth on the knoll, past tombstones set in odd patterns, and took their seats under the tent across from a blanket of artificial grass. Rain drizzled down from the gray sky. The coffin was set on two ropes held by four grave diggers, day laborers for Elijah from time to time. The preacher asked the Lord to be with Elijah's family, reassured them that Elijah was in a better place than those who remained and, in a low voice, said the Lord's prayer.

The service was over. Family and friends milled around awhile and a few out-of-town guests laughed and joked trying to renew old acquaintances. The task of lowering the coffin was left up to the undertaker and his helpers. The four men eased up on the ropes, dropping the coffin slowly down into the red clay. The undertaker guided the coffin with a broom handle, letting it slush into the muddy water at the bottom of the grave. The men shoveled dirt back into the grave and covered it with topsoil embedded in clover. They placed the sprays of flowers girls had carried out on top of the grave, and the undertaker took a small hammer and pounded a temporary marker into the ground, gave his helpers three dollars apiece, and left.

The grave diggers had stayed in a shed near the graveyard during the funeral service, talking, drinking beer, telling jokes. They didn't share the family's grief. One by one they had talked about Elijah and the times they had spent working for him, their memories of him. They had agreed on several things: he had worked them hard, taking their smoking tobacco away from them early in the morning, not giving it back until the day's work was done, paying a dollar-a-day for hard labor working in tobacco, milking cows in all kinds of weather, shucking corn, building fences, and putting foot logs across the creek. They talked about how he was big in the church, claiming to be a Christian, yet making social calls on some of the wives of his sharecroppers while the men were working in the fields. They had never been in his house, never eaten at his table. Sometimes he would load them in the back of a truck and take them to the store for ice cream, even once to the County Fair in Proctorville. Breaking out another six-pack of longnecks, they grabbed their shovels and piled the dirt back into the grave slowly watching the coffin disappear as the slick, red clay filled the hole. Hurrying now as twilight came, they laughed and joked, calling each other vile names, planning their trip over to Fat Watts' beer joint where they would join other carousers passing away the rest of the day. One of them summed up their feeling when he said Elijah had it coming.

In the distance, across the Ohio River, a crow's sad voice penetrated the mist. Cows lingering along the hillside flats began to wander toward the barns. Smoke from a burning tobacco bed curled up from the hollow toward Greasy Ridge. Down in the valley where the Indian Guyan Creek flowed, muskrats dodged steel traps and fish slithered around the trot lines.

# Reunion at Stony Point

Stony Point School was a typical one-room school built in Guyan Township, Ohio, in the early 1870s. It sat on a knoll at the top of what we called the "Stony Point" hill on State Route 218 five miles north of Scottown. You could not have found a better place for a school. It was close to the main road inland from the Ohio River connecting Gallipolis and Ironton. Many children lived within walking distance. Older kids rode horses, as did the teachers. It sat high, where during recess, you could look out over the valley and Indian Guyan Creek. Hazelnuts grew among the tall oaks nearby on the grounds. Teachers took the kids on field trips to the ridge where peach orchards lay and

Author's collection

*Sardis one-room school stands near the site of Stony Point. In northern Ohio, many one-room schools were made of brick, evidencing the difference in the regional economies.*

to watch corn ground into flour at Chapman's Mill. Stony Point could have been a model for a Currier and Ives print or Winslow Homer's painting, *Crack The Whip.* In the spring, the blue blossoms of wild Sweet Williams waved in the breeze. In the fall, hickory nuts and walnuts fell among the golden leaves. In the winter, a fire crackled inside the pot-bellied stove. Children worked on slates, memorized poems, and learned about casting out nines and what an aught was.

My Dad, his brothers and sisters and, later, my older brothers and sister went to school there. Stony Point was a short walk from my house, and I used to go there and look for artifacts—a slate board, a pencil, a pocket-knife, a marble, a piece of glass—anything that might reflect the fact that this was once a scene of gaiety, learning, and an occasional fight. The building was gone by that time, razed by a fire set by a person who didn't want Emma Moore to have a job teaching there. I never found anything except a few rocks and the residue of horse-drawn scrapers that had made the sharp turn at the top of the hill more amenable to horses, buggies, and cars.

Duane Null collection

*John, George, Virgil, and Mary Null, Webster Road, Patriot, Ohio, circa 1910. The boys play marbles at home while their sister looks on; marbles was primarily a boy's game. Many played "for keeps" at school—if a teacher didn't catch them.*

In the summer of 1928, the alumni of Stony Point organized a reunion to be held on the school grounds. The golden tassels of the corn in the fertile bottoms of Indian Guyan Creek were silent. Dog days had set in and small pools of muddy water nestled against the brown dirt banks. Snake doctors maneuvered up and down, stopping to rest on the purple ironweed blossoms. The tobacco in the flats along the hillsides was yellow and tough, ready for cutting. It was deep summer in the valley. A small congregation of people were gathered on the Stony Point school grounds. Women dressed in cotton print dresses and homemade bonnets worked about the long table placed in the shade of a silver maple tree. Men in high-collar shirts with gartered sleeves stood in small groups, talked and laughed. Children romped in the woods nearby, ran around trees, tumbled in the dirt. Babies on pallets slept in the shade.

The sun rolled down toward the western skyline of trees and shadows got longer. Several men and older boys carried folding chairs up the bank and set them up in uneven rows in front of a podium. Everyone gathered about and took their places in the chairs. The women stirred the heavy air with fans that had Stevers Funeral Home written on them. The dignitaries in wool suits sat facing the crowd. An old man stood, walked to the podium and prayed. A quartet sang, "Amazing Grace, how sweet the sound." Dust stirred up by passing cars on the gravel road below the point settled on the ironweeds that grew along the ditches. Cicadas in the woods above took turns grinding out their fitting, lonesome sounds. Grasshoppers shuffled in and out among the trampled leaves of grass. Yellow butterflies darted back and forth searching for nectar among the milkweed pods. Young men, apart from the ceremony, sat on the running boards of cars parked along the roads, smoked Camels, and sipped on paper cups of lemonade. Horses tied to fence posts strained to pull themselves toward strands of wild broom sedge that grew up through small stones by the edge of the road.

John Fowler, a former student and teacher at Stony Point, wrote a poem for the occasion, *Reunion At Stony Point.* In its own melancholy way, the poem seemed to be influenced by a poem called *Forty Years Ago* that was in McGuffey's Fifth Reader, a work most schoolchildren of the time had memorized. Fowler was an archetype of the old country schoolmaster. He was a strong, serious man well-educated for the time. He could handle the ruffians who came to school to start trouble, and he knew how to be kind and gentle to the tiny, scared first-graders. This was a time of little irony, and the content of school books was replete with essays and poems about death, sadness, and the belief in eternal truths. They were taught that good outlasted bad; that the kid who skipped school without his parent's permission and went swimming drowned; that the kid who helped his mother with the chores was rewarded with a pleasant surprise.

John Fowler walked behind the lectern and read from his poem:

> *The old school-house is on the hill*
> *Upon the same school ground;*
> *But the great trees that shadowed it,*
> *They're nowhere to be found.*
> *The lovely groves are cleared away,*
> *And Oh, we miss them so;*
> *But things have changed so very much*
> *Since fifty-years ago.*
>
> *The public road that passed the place*
> *Has changed to new surveys,*
> *It's now a graded, graveled road*
> *Improved in many ways.*
> *The hills and dales we used to roam*
> *Where the hawthorn used to grow,*
> *Have lost their natural beauty*
> *Of fifty-years ago.*

Author's collection

*Refreshment stand, Guyan Valley School House, 1908.*

*Many of the dear schoolmasters*
*Have long since passed away,*
*But their noble work is living*
*In responsive hearts today.*
*We, like autumn leaves, are falling*
*As the seasons come and go,*
*We cannot meet in school again*
*As fifty-years ago.*

The crowd was moved to reflection when Mr. Fowler left the stage and walked down to shake hands. The author gave copies of the poem to all who wanted them. After a long period of visiting among one another, the crowd began to stir about, gathered up their children and dinner accouterments, and meandered to cars and horse-drawn conveyances parked along the side of the dusty road. The muffled sounds of bells came from the flats along the escarpments as cows began to slip down narrow traces toward barns below. The westward sky darkened with black clouds, shutting off the evening sun rays.

The people hurried to their farms up and down the valley and back on the ridges. The autumn of 1928 approached, unrecognized. An old woman in the back seat of a car stared for a minute at a printed folder she had picked up at the reunion and stuck it inside a battered copy of McGuffey's sixth reader. Down through the long years, the little booklet with *Fifty Years Ago* printed inside remained a memento that was kept among the faded souvenirs of baby pictures, newspaper clippings, post cards, report cards, and locks of hair.

*The children now are much the same,*
*Life's blood is just as warm,*
*The noon-day sun shines just as bright*
*On every field and farm.*
*The birds sing just as sweetly, too,*
*The buds and grasses grow;*
*But things have changed so very much*
*Since fifty years ago.*
*We remember well our childhood,*
*Its songs were full of praise;*
*We recall the joys of school life,*
*Its hallowed, happy days.*
*And when we're done with earth, we hope*
*To meet with those we know,*
*The dear school-mates, we loved so well,*
*Some fifty years ago.*

*Author's note (from original copy)*

NOTE—The little contribution of verse was written in commemoration of the Stony Point School in Guyan Township, Gallia County, Ohio, and in grateful remembrance of the Devoted, Upright People of that community, and in Fond Remembrance of the Fine Student Body of the renowned Stony Point School.

AUTHOR—John Harrison Fowler was born July 1, 1868, and was reared to manhood in sight of the "old school-house." Early in life, he engaged in farming and became inured to the hard labor and privations of pioneer life. He attended the Stony Point School from 1875 to 1885. In 1887, at the age of 18, he began teaching and continued in the profession until 1927, when he retired. He received a state life certificate in 1928. A resident of his native state and county all his life, Fowler's teaching experience of 32 years was all rendered in the schools of Gallia County.

# Mail Pouch

In the late 19th century, Wheeling, West Virginia, was an entrepreneur's dream. Wheeling had been a stopover town on the National Road west for 50 years. Boats on the Ohio River waited their turns to unload goods and people at the wharfboat. Jobs were there in the iron, steel, and glass factories, and small merchants prospered. Immigrants late of Ellis Island mixed with third-generation natives. At night, the taverns, theaters, and dance halls were gay with revelry. Prostitution and gambling complemented the town's hustle and bustle as it did in other boomtowns. Wheeling also had the distinction of being the center for the production of stogies (cheap cigars) in the United States. In 1879, brothers Aaron and Samuel Bloch began to roll stogies as a sideline to their wholesale grocery and dry goods business on Main Street. Observing that scrap stogie wrapper clippings were used by some as chewing tobacco, the Bloch brothers decided to add flavor to these clippings, package, and sell them. It was a revolutionary move for the industry, and West Virginia Mail Pouch chewing tobacco was born.

The product's popularity soon spread throughout the Midwest, and the words "West Virginia" were dropped. Ever the promoter, Aaron Bloch, in about 1900, suggested the idea of advertising on barns, adding the slogan, "For chewing and smoking." A few years later, a sign painter changed the slogan to, "Treat Yourself to the Best." Painting this large yellow, black, and white logo on barns soon took on a life of its own. These were images that fit the American character. Painted on thousands of barns throughout the Midwest, the signs were like the people who rode past them in buggies and cars:  rural, indepen-

Author's collection

*A Mail Pouch barn on State Route 7 in Gallia County, Ohio.*

dent, rugged, wholesome, and colorful. It was as though an advertising logo had risen from the soil itself. In these days of family farms, barns were not just utility buildings to cure and store farm produce and house domestic animals. They were places where social activities took place. Men gathered in barns in winter and summer to socialize, trade knives, and make deals. There among the horses and cows that meandered in and out, away from the primness of the houses where women dominated, men were able to talk about the scriptures, play cards, tell stories, smoke and chew tobacco with abandon, and, on occasion, pass around a pint of Old Grand Dad. Barns were, moreover, places where children played. They gamboled in the haylofts, climbed the tierpoles, teased wasps and snakes, and threw corncobs and rotten eggs at one another.

In the early part of this century, before World War I and the popularity of cigarettes, chewing tobacco and cigars were the primary tobacco products. In the culture of working men, farmers, coal miners, cotton pickers, factory workers, truck drivers, buskers, and drifters, chewing tobacco was a convenient way to get an intake of nicotine.

One could work and chew at the same time. Unlike cigars, which were more expensive, gave off smoke and ashes, and required manipulation by hand, one could chew anywhere—in the wind, in the fields, in the factories, or indoors. Chewing was easy to learn and, in most social circles, acceptable. All chewers had to do was shove a moderate amount of tobacco, cut from a plug or pinched from scrap, into their jaws between cheek and gum and let the juices slowly flow. One could go for hours without spitting. Farmers in forgiving climates grew their own. Formed into twists and aged, chunks of homemade tobacco cut off twists with pocket knives were offered up to others as symbols of friendship. Spitting even had status. Some men spat with great accuracy by holding two fingers against their lips. The ability to spit several feet and hit a target became a skill young men sought to achieve. County fairs offered contests with prizes awarded to long distance-spitters. In a fist fight, tobacco might be spat in an opponent's eye and warm spit was a home remedy for ear aches. Brass spittoons—also called cuspidors—were everywhere. In the great saloons, public buildings, stores, trains, barber shops, and homes—wherever men congregated—fine golden spittoons were necessary accouterments.

In the 1920s as cars and roads increased sharply, road crews of two men per truck fanned out across the land to grace thousands of barns with the Mail Pouch logo. Maurice Zimmerman from Washington Court House, Ohio, was one of these crew members from the early years. He hired on in 1925. Using a Model T Ford truck with side curtains, he and his partner set out from Syracuse, New York. They worked their way west on main roads leasing barn space and painting signs along the way. Using six-inch brushes called mops and overalls called skins, these barn "lizards" wore the same overalls until they were stiff and crusted, then threw them away. They worked the year around if the weather was suitable. In the wintertime, they wore five-buckle arctics over their work shoes. One summer Zimmerman took his wife along, and they lived in a tent. While he painted barns, she canned blueberries picked from the fields and cooked on a three-burner portable stove. He continued to work for the Bloch Brothers through

*Abandoned barn in winter, Lawrence County, Ohio.*

Author's collection

World War II and later was a partner with the most famous of all the barn painters, Harley Warrick of Belmont, Ohio. Warrick, who until his death at 76 in 2000, built Mail Pouch replicas and painted barns for exhibitions, gets credit for much of the logo's lasting appeal.

He was born in a tobacco barn in Belmont County, Ohio, in 1924. There, among the steep hills and rolling pastures of the eastern Appalachian plateau, he developed an independence and firmness of spirit reminiscent of the cowboys who worked the great western plains. In his youth, Harley pitched in with the farm work that meant survival. His early milieu was one where neighbors exchanged produce and labor with one another as needed.

Women walked the small parcels of land in early spring gathering wild greens with a butcher knife and a dish pan. Hogs and steers were butchered for meat. Rabbits and squirrels were taken from the woods and dressed for dinner tables. Riffles in Captina Creek gave up cat fish and suckers. Harley and his friends gigged Frogs and pulled turtles out by their tails from underwater lairs. They caught raccoons, opossums, and foxes with steel traps. The Warrick family picked grapes, raspberries, blackberries, and persimmons, ate them raw or put up jelly for winter. Hunting and gathering were part of existence. No government help was forthcoming, and none was expected. The biggest event Harley Warrick remembers from childhood happened in the summer of 1936. After the hay was put up in August, his father loaded the family into a Model T Ford and took them to the Ohio State Fair in Columbus.

Harley Warrick graduated from Madison High School in 1942. He, along with thousands of others from rural Appalachia, headed north to work. He went to Canton, moved in with his sister, and walked the cold streets to and from the Timkin Roller Bearing factory. He helped Timkin produce tank turrets until, at 18, he joined the Army. After basic training, he took a troop ship to Europe and, among others, received battle stars for the Remagen Bridge Crossing and the Battle of the Bulge. When Harley returned home in 1946, his family had moved to a farm near Londonderry in Guernsey County. The barn there had a Mail Pouch sign on it that caught his attention each day when he went to help milk the cows. One cold February day, a crew from Mail Pouch came by to repaint the sign. Delbert Duffey, a nephew of one of the original contractors and one of the painters, told Harley the crew could use another man. Harley went to the house, threw a change of clothes and a few packs of Pall Malls in his old Army duffel bag, climbed into a 1937 Chevrolet panel truck, and headed out State Route 22, the William Perry Highway, toward Toledo. He didn't return for six months. Harley had no idea that he was starting a 40-year career that would take him across hundreds of nondescript two-lane roads from Missouri to New York, from Michigan to Tennessee. No thought that he would become one of America's foremost folk artists who would one day be commissioned to paint a barn for ABC TV newsman, Ted Koppel.

Out on the road in the post-World War II boom, before Eisenhower and the interstates, Harley Warrick was a quick learner. Following a band of company men who traded farmers supplies of tobacco, magazine subscriptions, or cash for the right to paint the side of a barn with their sales logo, he and his partner moved from barn to barn with their ladders and paint. Using dead reckoning to fix horizontal and vertical axes, they could finish a job in three hours or less. Finding the center of the area to be painted by counting the roof beams, they started with the P in "Pouch" and finished the word moving right. Going back to the center again, they painted to the left. The same procedure was used for the remaining words. Each man was paid $32.00 for a six-day week and they paid their own expenses. A picture of the barn was sent to the Bloch Brothers to verify its completion and size.

Harley and his partners over the years took to the highways up and down the land, young men in search of a living and adventure. They spent their nights in cheap hotels, boarding houses, or in the backs of their trucks. Harley has fond memories of a boarding house in Spencer, West Virginia. An old lady ran the place where a room and meals could be had for $1.75 a day. He went back there anytime he was in the area and, on summer evenings, gigged bull frogs from a creek nearby. Legs from the frogs, cooked up by the house owner, made tasty nighttime snacks. In other towns, paint crews would meet on weekends and, like a bunch of thirsty cowboys out on a cattle drive, find a local beer joint and have a few beers. Sometimes, one of the painters would get in a ruckus and wind up sleeping it off in jail. But when Monday morning came they got out early, picked up a six-pack and some lunch meat, and headed off to the next barn.

Harley did get back to Belmont County long enough to get married when he was 27. Cutting back on his traveling, he was able to get home almost every weekend. Still, his wife, the mother of his two children, complained about being alone. She told him either to change jobs or wives. Harley, figuring another wife would be easier to find than another job, chose work. Harley remarried and, this time, his career moved forward with few complaints.

The next 40 years gave Harley Warrick a lifetime of chances to polish his skills and work the road. Never using a stencil for a crutch, his calibrated eyeballs helped him fix the sign lettering into perfect, but appropriately rough, form. In a good year, he painted up to 700 barns; 20,000 in his career. In recent years, he, together with the sign, has become well known beyond the borders of Belmont County. Harley has a certificate of recognition for painting a barn at the Smithsonian Institution of Performing Arts of Montreal, a National Agricultural Award from Governor Jay Rockefeller of West Virginia, a community service award from Wheeling, life membership in the West Virginia Tobacco Growers Association, and an honorary degree of Hard Knocks from Alderson-Broaddus College. He has been featured on television by *Good Morning America*, Charles Kuralt's *On The Road*, and selected P.M. Magazine shows. The *Smithsonian, Wall Street Journal, Ohio Farmer, Ohio, Grit, National Enquirer, Goldenseal,* and *Ripley's Believe It Or Not* have presented Harley to the world. Renowned artist Ray Day of Missouri has honored him and the sign with a limited print called "Fresh

*Barns sheltered tobacco, hay, and cattle. They were social centers where men gathered to drink, deal, talk, smoke, chew, cuss, and wait for the rain to stop before they went back to the fields. Modest women stayed away from barns.*

Author's collection

Paint, A Tribute to Harley." National Public Radio has interviewed him with the sounds of a paint brush slapping in the background.

True to his character, Harley remains humble. Comparing his skills to a ditch digger, he says it never was anything more than a job to him. Like most successful ventures, however, there was always a love for the work itself. One who travels to Belmont and seeks Harley out will find him in his well-appointed workshop, quid of Mail Pouch in his jaw, making Mail Pouch miniatures: plaques, birdhouses, and kitchen whatnots. Finding his religion in the wonders of nature, he revealed that he goes to church twice on Sundays: once to take his wife, the other to pick her up. Harley, ever the political conservative, is impatient with most attempts by government officials to interfere with life's natural flow. He had a personal altercation a few years ago in the Belmont Post Office with his Congressman, the late Wayne Hayes, and saw no sense in Lady Bird Johnson's Highway Beautification Act of 1965 which forced the Bloch Brothers to limit their barn advertisements. And of his recent fame, his belief is that he just kept doing what he always did, and the world came around his way.

The Mail Pouch barn signs that Harley and others painted were always large and rustic. There were thousands of them standing against the elements along the two-lane roads that crisscrossed the USA before the interstates. With an occasional touch up of new paint and a few board replacements, each one lasted for decades. Holes from stray shotgun pellets only enhanced their dignity. These were barns that marked the trails, images that gave directions to lost motorists between farms and villages. The black, white, and yellow letters were symbols of adventures and good times that lay ahead a few more miles as on the mother road west, US 66. The Mail Pouch barns are representative of the manner in which the human mind forever holds pleasant memories while suppressing melancholia. Like an old bluegrass ballad, the crispy pulley bone from mother's fried chicken, the anticipation of a long, hot afternoon of summer play along dusty sidewalks, or a ride in the back seat of father's Ford V/8, the old, fading barns evoke a reverie that few images of popular culture can touch.

# A Tombstone for Simon Davis

I watched three men load the homemade slab of concrete on my toy wagon. It was a warm afternoon in late June, and, although I was only seven-years old, I was going with these men, one of whom was my father, on an unusual summer adventure. I thought they probably let me go only because they were using my wagon. And I was afraid they were going to tear it up with that heavy slab, too. I was also scared because the slab was a tombstone, and they were going to take it back on a hill and place it by a grave. I had been to cemeteries and seen tombstones before, but this was different.

As we left the driveway from my house, I noticed that the inscription on the slab was simply, **Simon Davis 1845 - 1915**. Simon Davis, I later learned, was a veteran of the Civil War who had lived on a hill farm near my house in southern Ohio. He had come there after the war and settled with his wife to make a living growing peaches. The sandy, limestone soil on the hills there was fertile ground for growing fruit.

One of the men in the group, James Clutter, had made the tombstone and was

*The grave of author's maternal grandmother, Buena Vista Lewis. She died at age 40, in 1905, giving birth to her eighth child, and is buried high on a hill near a few other graves. The graveyard is fenced in to keep cattle out and is seldom visited.*

Author's collection

the instigator of the task at hand. Clutter, as a youth, had spent a lot of time loafing around the Davis farm. He had gone there many times to get water and peaches, and, from these pleasant experiences of his youth, he felt he owed Simon Davis one last favor. No decent person should be buried 25 years and have no grave marker; in the hill country, this couldn't be.

Simon Davis seemed eccentric to the community, especially to James Clutter. Living way back on a hill kept him out of daily contact with those people who were on the main roads where peddlers, mail carriers, and others traveled. Davis had told the young Clutter that he wanted to be buried sitting up so he could watch his peach orchard. Davis was a Civil War veteran, and he was typical of the last of the frontier men. He had no confidence in government at any level. Davis was just as skeptical of the Federal Government as he was of the township trustees. When asked once by a neighbor if he got any mail, Davis replied, "nothing but a damned government circular." In a community where most people shared the fellowship of one-room schools and churches, Simon Davis lived on the periphery of the social mainstream.

I followed the men along the gravel road which ran in front of my house. They took turns pulling and pushing the wagon and holding onto the slab so it didn't slip off. After about a quarter mile we left the road, headed across a pasture field, and crossed the creek. The going was much harder when we left the road. They had to pull, shove, and wiggle the tiny wagon back and forth to move it along through the tall grass and ruts and through the soft sand in the creek bed. I still had the queasy feeling that they were going to break the wagon down.

They moved into the woods and on up the hillside. The trail in the woods was narrow, with tree limbs extending into the path. There were vines and ferns and always the possibility that a snake might be disturbed. I was scared of snakes. I knew they were bad news, because I had seen my mother take a hoe and chop their heads off. I never touched one, live or dead.

*Properly marked graves are important in Appalachian culture. Graveyard, Mingo County, West Virginia.*

About halfway up the hill, one of the men who was carrying a mattock saw a box turtle in his path. He drew the mattock back and smashed it into the turtle's back. I felt sad that he would kill a harmless turtle. It just laid there with its head and legs sticking out. Its eyes never closed. They moved on with no hesitation, through the heavy brush, up and over the moss-covered rocks, past the white violets that grew in places where the sun could get to. Walking behind the others, I had to dodge the limbs that whipped back as the men walked past them.

The group moved on rapidly up the hill and finally moved out of the thicket into the cleared flat that bordered along the woods. They moved on through the broom sage and ironweeds and, once again, turned up the hill until they reached the top. I felt like I was a long way from home when I looked over the valleys. In the distance to the south, a small airplane motor droned in stark contrast to the softer sounds of birds and insects.

Clutter signaled that we had arrived at the grave site, and the men directed the wagon to a spot alongside the grave. My father was carrying a container with water, and the other man had a small sack of cement mixed with sand. They dug a rectangular hole about eight inches deep and filled it with the green mixture of concrete, sand, and water. They placed the slab in the wet concrete carefully so that it was positioned properly and stable, then brushed the dirt off their hands and sat down to rest. James Clutter lit a Camel cigarette. Everyone joked and laughed, now that the work was over and their task completed. Simon Davis had a headstone, and they all knew it would be there for a long time.

*Monuments in a Fulks' family graveyard with birth dates going back to 1835. A Civil War veteran, GAR, is buried here. In the early part of the 19th century, families buried their dead on the farm and still counted them in the family. Sharing burial space with the poor, graves were kept up, and children were taught not to step on a grave.*

Author's collection

# Dark Bluff—
# The History of an Ohio River Village

The driver slapped the reins against the backs of his team. The horses lurched against their collars, the farm wagon screeched and twisted, iron tires scraping against the rocks jutting into the foot-deep ruts. Up and up, on Luther Suthers Hill, the driver guided his 1000-pound, tarpaulin-covered load of dark, air-cured tobacco. He pressed on, horses snorting vapor, as they passed the white frame Church of Christ where, nearly 50 years earlier, one of General Morgan's Confederate raiders shot and killed a Greasy Ridge doctor as he made his rounds by horseback. Another half-mile gained the top of the hill and a crossing of the high ridge road that ran northeastward for 40 miles, separating the Indian Guyan Creek farms from the Ohio River. Tugging hard, the driver steadied the team as the wagon yawed down the winding descent and, going over the Simms Run covered bridge, entered the port village of Crown City. Within a few minutes, the cargo was unloaded at the "loose leaf barn," the American Tobacco Company warehouse, near the river. On a late autumn morning in 1911, the village's 300 residents were taking their bearings on the day to come.

Draymen with mule-drawn carts shuttled between the wharf boat and John Rankin's general store on Main Street. Crates of fruit, cross-cut saws, nails, lamp oil, skillets, and nostrums filled its shelves and counters. Farm families, in for Saturday trading, exchanged lard, eggs, butter, and black Minorca chickens for sugar, hard candy, and Battle Ax chewing tobacco. Loafers—an odd assortment of septuagenarian war veterans, coal diggers, and mule skinners, as rugged as the terrain

Gerald Sutphin collection

*In the 19th century, steamboats like the Homer Smith made runs from New Orleans to Pittsburgh, loading and unloading goods and passengers at hundreds of wharf boats in villages like Crown City. Draymen waited to haul products unloaded by roustabouts up to the general stores. One of the author's grandfathers used to haul hogs by boat to market in Cincinnati and come home with a pocketful of 20-dollar gold pieces.*

they had whipped—lounged on the corners. At the intersection of Charles and Crown streets, tellers with gartered sleeves manned the cages of the Crown City Bank. On the corner opposite the impressive, two-story brick bank, the Simms brothers, Coon and Eustace, were busily stocking their new venture in general merchandise. Buggies, expresses, and much rarer Model T Fords and Maxwells were parked in the business section. Riley Cart's Florence Hotel on Main Street provided homey bed-and-board to river travelers and hot, family-style meals to all comers. In his Charles Street office, Dr. Edwin M. Martindill was seeing patients. For 50 cents he would take a blood pressure reading and fill a little white envelope with pills. A brick school, to accommodate grades one through eleven, was under construction. The village also had a cooper's shop, a livery stable, a saloon, an undertaker, a gristmill, and law and order in the shape of a town marshal. Although the river had made the village, the slow-traveling packet boats were beginning to give way to the great wonder of the era, the motorcar. The center of town, once on the riverfront, had moved three blocks west, to Crown Street.

Three generations earlier, the river was vital. Wolves, bears, and bison had drunk there for thousands of years. Grouse, doves, and turkeys nested along the shore. Bluebells bloomed on the high banks. Shawnees had canoed the river waters and camped beside creeks that later were called Swan, Sugar, and Two-mile. Immigrants crossing the Alleghenies learned that a flatboat on the Ohio could take its passengers the 290-odd miles down river from Pittsburgh in a few days. Land was cheap, and the Scotch-Irish drifters were hungry for a place. The rich bottomland, the hills with timber, coal and limestone, and a strong bluff that jutted into the river were natural lures. The Shawnees were crowded out, and the banditti that prowled the river were scared off. Between 1800 and 1840 the village took hold and began to grow.

Author's collection

*The Crown City bank building today. When railroads and cars replaced river boats, Crown City died.*

The surrounding township, Guyan, was surveyed, and two or more schools operated through the winter months. Hiram Rankin and others became prominent landowners. By 1850 more than 400 people lived in the township, and the village had grown to about 50. Settlers, who worked small farms inland along the Indian Guyan Creek valley, walked or drove horses and wagons across the hill to the river to trade, call for their mail, and socialize. Thomas Bay owned the biggest and best piece of river frontage, so the village came to be called Bays Bottom. By 1847 a post office had been established, steam packets made regular stops, and johnboaters rowed toward destinations up and down the river on both shores.

Soon after the Civil War, Postmaster Charles A. Seidler orchestrated efforts to give the village a new name. Crown Point, first suggested, was denied because it was already taken by a village near Dayton. Crown City seemed a logical alternative and was accepted and made official in 1870. As the 20th century approached, a network of primitive roads and trails ran north and south along the river and east of Walnut Street, in and over the nearby hills, along the distant ridges, and up the many hollows. One-room schools, with picturesque names like Stony Point and Brush College, dotted the hills and valleys. The Methodist Church moved into a new building on Charles Street in 1874. Steamboats like *Buckeye State, Queen City*, and *Henry M. Stanley* plied the river, with Crown City among their ports of call. In 1888, the Ohio River Railroad came down the opposite shore, increasing ferryboat traffic between the village and Greenbottom, West Virginia. Boat crews and trainmen brought news of the world's doings into the village, and the postmaster read it aloud from his office steps. And on a hot September day in 1895, Governor William McKinley, 52-years old and an unannounced candidate for president, addressed a crowd of 5,000 on the Soldier's Reunion Grounds near the narrows.

The culture of the river had a deep effect on life in Crown City. Strangers came in, stayed a few hours or days, and moved on. They brought new ideas that intermingled with provincial values. Free from

Author's collection

*First grade class, Mercerville School, Gallia County, Ohio. Kathryn Gothard, teacher, upper left; author, far right, second row, circa 1940 . At least two children are barefooted, more for comfort than because they were poor. The "no shoes, no shirt, no learning" rule came later.*

the restraints of local ties, men off the river were eager participants in the brawling, drinking, and gambling of the wharf boat district. Crown City entrepreneurs, quick to sense a chance at moneymaking, provided the necessary accommodations. Villagers also found work and the promise of adventure on the river. Men became deck hands, mud clerks, and mates. Women were taken on as riverboat cooks. From Louisville, Memphis, and St. Louis, they brought back department store goods and modern ideas. Change was inevitable.

Countering the challenge of outside influences that threatened to make Crown City the same as any other place was the preserved memory of events that gave the community a singular character. Craig Pike told the story of Jim Lewis, village marshal and undertaker, who crossed the deep swale of Simms Run to Buzzards Roost to serve an arrest warrant on a local character named Bogan Canaday. When Lewis found him, Canaday knew what was up, but, nothing personal, said he wasn't ready to be arrested. Without a word, Lewis turned around and left. About three months later, Canaday appeared, saying, "Jim, I'm ready to go." He did his time in the local jail, got out, and went on about his business. Lewis allowed Canaday to save face, when doing otherwise would serve no real purpose; he had made his own rules and avoided making an enemy.

Then there was Vinton Armstrong Rankin, saloon-keeper, riverboat pilot, merchant, and the village's most prominent resident. A huge, round-faced man who wore a cropped beard and mustache, Rankin had been both a steamboat man and a Yankee soldier during the Civil War. One time, a drummer—a traveling salesman—announced in Rankin's riverfront saloon that he had left a barrel of flour down on the wharf boat that would belong to anyone who could carry it home. Rankin vowed that there were women in Crown City who handled heavier loads than that. When the drummer told him to bring one on, Rankin stepped outside and whistled loudly. His sister appeared, and Rankin told her that the flour was hers if she could carry it home. She did.

Some of the schools in the Crown City hinterland retained a rowdy, frontier aspect. Inland teachers had to be tough to survive. When Alf Dillon told a ruffian at Gregory School to put his knife in his pocket and keep it there, the youth defied him. Dillon picked up a poker by the potbellied stove and advanced toward the boy's desk. A second later the knife was pocketed, and Dillon resumed the recitations. School board politics also could generate hard feelings. Emma Moore and her friends voted the wrong way in the 1929 board election. Her school assignment, Stony Point, burnt down before school started. Two years later, when she was assigned to teach at Gregory Elementary, it, too, burnt down.

One-room schools were available to all who chose to complete eight years, but there was no high school and no higher education for teachers. Henry Swindler, a farmer who lived on Indian Guyan Creek near Chapman's Mill, left money in his estate about 1890 to build an academy. The school, called Lincoln High, was located on Williams Ridge a half-mile west of Crown City. A summer-school curriculum to prepare prospective teachers for the county teachers examination was offered. The school suffered from lack of enrollment, and, within a few years, it closed. The building was moved six miles north to Mercerville. Students walked in and came on horseback from Crown City and other nearby villages. The first principal, Charles E. Price, recruited teachers, developed a curriculum, formed a literary society, and organized pie suppers. Diversions included debates and baseball games and flirting in the modest manner of the times. Some schools and teachers failed, but there were always diligent tobacco farmers along the creeks and on the ridges who were willing to support new efforts.

*Helen Null in a tobacco field ready for harvest, Gallia County, Ohio, 1973. Southern Ohio farmers grew burley tobacco, high quality leaf. They burnt the beds, seeded them, set the plants, hoed and plowed the fields, topped and suckered the tobacco, took it in, hung it in barns to cure, graded it, tied it into hands, and hauled it to markets in Huntington, West Virginia, and Maysville, Kentucky. For chewing, they twisted their own.*

Duane Null collection

Burley tobacco, the golden leaf that satisfied smokers, chewers, and snuff dippers, was the cash crop in Guyan Township and a boon to Crown City merchants and traders. Each season's harvest was prefigured on a cold, February day when men went into the dark woods to cut trees to burn a tobacco bed. Selected green timber logs from locust, oak, walnut, and pine trees were cut with crosscut saws. The logs were snaked by a team of horses to a large rectangular area near the foot of the hill. Fired by kerosene, the logs burnt through the day and into the night, killing fertile weed seeds. The soft ashes that remained were mixed with the rich dirt to provide a plant bed for the fine tobacco seeds.

Plants were set by hand in the small bottom fields or in new ground grubbed out in hillside flats. Men worked the fields behind one-horse cultivators. Dirt was loosened and weeds cut with gooseneck hoes. In deep summer each plant was topped and suckered over and over again by families whose hands soon became black with gummy sap. Worms were plucked off and smashed underfoot. The yellow and brown plants were cut in early September and hung beneath barn rafters to cure. As Thanksgiving approached, the tobacco stalks were stripped as the leaves came "in case"—soft and easy to handle—and sorted into grades called brightleaf, lugs, trash, redleaf, and tips. The tobacco was tied into "hands," pressed, and sent off to market. In 1911, a farmer who harvested several acres might have 3,000 pounds of tobacco worth 12 cents a pound. Three-hundred-sixty dollars in hard money. Most had smaller crops. Sharecroppers split their harvests and often ended the year owing their half to the landowner. Day laborers, who had worked all summer for a quarter a day, were lucky to get bed, board, and roll-your-own Bugler tobacco in exchange for help with winter chores. Some, in dire straits, went on relief or to the county poorhouse. Many times, farmers just took their tobacco checks to the grocer or the banker and turned it over to them to pay off bills and notes, maybe holding a little out for Christmas. Some got their checks cashed, got drunk, and lost it all in a poker game in Huntington, West Virginia. Then the whole process started over.

Tobacco farming in Guyan Township was basic to the economy. But few made any real money from it. Bottomland with rich, sandy soil was scarce, and even a good crop might be flooded out. New ground in hillside flats had to be grubbed out by hand with axes and mattocks. A good tobacco crop, milk and cream to sell, hogs to

*Vernacular house, northern Appalachia, unidentified child.*

butcher, raspberries and blackberries to can, cane for molasses, and a few truck crops to market through the summer enabled those who were industrious to live. Simple, cheap furniture, tools, clothes, and food prevailed. Life and nature were one. Cold, heat, rain, and darkness were thwarted by simple, frame houses. Farm animals were fed, milked, and butchered in muddy barnyards. Half-frozen calves and lambs were thawed out in front of kitchen fireplaces. Men, women, and children made their way along darkened paths through the seasons to putrid outhouses. In times of sickness, chamber pots were emptied into frozen creeks.

Except for the human bonds and character that hardship, family, schools, and religion fostered, the inland culture was low and primitive. The only moral outrage against tobacco came from a small sect of Holiness Church members with little or no community influence. Although most men, and some women and children, gave in to the boredom and smoked or chewed the poison weed, successful preachers knew that their dark suits and new cars depended on a good year for tobacco and stuck to tried-and-true themes of lust, drunkenness,

and other forms of depravity. While most farmers subsisted, the owners of bottomland along the river north of Crown City, and a few
merchants, were able to get money ahead. The society of the inland
farmers and village dwellers was that described in Wilbur J. Cash's
classic dissection of the former Confederacy, *The Mind of the South*.
Only political accident and the run of the river had placed them in
the North. Music was made by fiddles, banjos, and guitars. They sang
songs about their mothers, death, and the grand reunion in heaven.
Families were clannish. Beans, cornbread, country ham, and potatoes
were staples; religion was primitive and fundamental; government
officeholders were not trusted; hospitality among their own kind was
a grand virtue. One could travel as far as Georgia and never encoun-
ter dissimilar values. The racial ethos was southern; black roustabouts
from the riverboats were never able to come ashore and socialize with
whites at Crown City. And the few blacks who entered Guyan Township from Virginia soon moved on to friendlier territory.

Summers of the years following World War I continued to bring
traveling circuses, showboats, and religious tent meetings to the village. The camp meeting, held for a week annually in the shade of the
black maple trees by the Methodist Church, was a big event for both
village and township residents. The church choir prepared special
music, and local misses took turns at the organ. The Athalia quartet,
sweat from the summer heat pouring down their faces, sang:

> *Pass me not, O gentle savior,*
> *Hear my humble cry;*
> *While on others thou art calling,*
> *Do not pass me by.*

Hymnody, and the plaintive licks struck on guitars and pianos, were
Crown City's spiritual armor against bereavement. Through the years
of hard times and primitive medicine, death was an intimate com-
panion. With little respite from tragedy, and a powerful belief that all

would be united again in the great beyond, funerals and graveside rites were ultimately solemn. John Stevers and his son, Lee, were the village undertakers. There they were, time after time, in the graveyard on the knoll, dressed in blue serge suits, directing the slow movements that grief requires for even the most hard born. And men grasping strong ropes, led by the undertaker guiding the coffin with a broom handle, would lower the body down into the poor, brown dirt. Preachers who pronounced these graveside sermons were part-time farmers who had limited knowledge of theology and mores beyond the Ohio Valley. But men of character like Ira Sheets and Napoleon Burnette inspired the efforts of those who sought to become more virtuous. Small-town roughnecks, thieves, and riffraff knew that their destiny was a hell that burnt on for eternity. Children, fools, and heathen from alien lands were forgiven, for they didn't know the difference anyway. With little room for negotiations, those who chose to work on Sunday, drink, carouse, lie, curse, or question the Bible's authority were set aside from the church folks.

Lester Stevers collection

*Lee Stevers, undertaker, horse-drawn hearse, Mercerville, Ohio, circa 1920. This type of hearse was used for funeral services on muddy roads even after motor coaches came to Appalachia.*

The sharp differences between the two groups were further focused by certain character traits found in the Appalachian people. Independent and stubborn by nature, individuals often found it hard to stay out of each other's territory. Whether it was a problem with stray cattle grazing in someone else's pasture, or the right to sit on a certain barstool, the propensity to solve problems with violence was all-too common.

During the hard times of 1931, 25-year-old Owen Hall of Gallipolis hired in as a steam shovel operator on a road job below Crown City. Away from his wife and child, with time on his hands and money in his pocket, "Peanut" Hall hung around with Miller resident Bethel Moore. On Saturday evening, June 13, Hall and Moore came up to Crown City in a Model A roadster. Moore was driving. They cruised around for a while, and Hall moved into the driver's seat. As he slowed for the sharp curve by the graveyard on State Route 7, a gunshot broke the evening calm. People rushing to the scene found Hall slumped in the car seat, blood coming from his mouth, a bullet hole in his right shoulder. He was dead before he got to a hospital in Huntington. Folks down there believe that whoever shot Hall apparently got the wrong man and that the shot was intended for Moore, who had a reputation for trouble. Just another killing. Using that word instead of murder because it implied that fate had caused them to switch places; and even if Moore had been shot, he had it coming. The coroner's inquest failed to turn up a suspect.

When Route 7 was completed from East Liverpool to Chesapeake, it followed Gallia Street through Crown City. The numbers of Ford Model T's and Model A's and other motorcars increased dramatically. Again, the center of town moved another block west and away from the river. Farm tractors and expensive Reo trucks began to appear, especially on the big farms along the river. Trips to Gallipolis and Huntington that once took four or five hours by horse-drawn vehicles or the river could be measured in minutes. Truckers made accessible the remote tobacco auctions in West Virginia and Kentucky where crops could be delivered, sold, and the money brought home the same day. The Crown City Bank had long since gone broke, and the out-of-town owners left several local investors to take the loss. Prohibition had closed down the saloons, leaving their business in the hands of boot-leggers. The high school closed in 1932, giving students the option of going over the hill six miles or down the river to Fairland in Lawrence County. River traffic continued to diminish, although showboats such as the *Majestic* still drew large crowds to the riverfront, where patrons could sit in the humid night air and see live shows like Ten Nights in a Barroom. But there were those who didn't give up on this village.

Among the population of 300 was Hobart Dillon, Crown City's most notable entrepreneur. In a place where residents settled for Fords and Chevrolets, Dillon drove a low-slung, monster Cord. Dillon was a distributor for Metallic X, an early version of super glue. For promo-tion, he put two speakers on the Cord's roof and hired Jimmie Fiddler and Lang Spires to sit in the back and play hillbilly music as he drove around. In 1932, when Myers Y. Cooper sought his third Republican nomination to the governor's office, he asked Dillon to chauffeur him across Ohio to his campaign appearances. Cooper lost anyway. When the curtain came down on prohibition in 1933, Hobart had a license, a restaurant that fronted on Route 7, and a back room stocked with cases of Wooden Shoe beer. People came from as far away as Gallipolis, Ironton, and Huntington. Cars lined the roadside for long distances north and south. Carry-out beer was iced down in cattle troughs set up outside the store.

By 1942, Route 7 had been straightened, raised from the floodplain, and moved westward out of the village. For the first time, through-traffic had a straight shot to Huntington. Young men joined or were drafted into the Army or Navy, sad to leave their families, but happy at the chance for adventure and, for the first time in their lives, easy money. On early June days, the soft cry of a turtledove could be heard through the stillness on Gallia Street. Children with ice cream cones rode their bikes, listening to the sound of rubber tires on dusty asphalt. Hershel Haskins—raised by his grandmother King, nicknamed "Cackle," and thereafter known as Cackle King—barbered beside a copper tank filled with scalding water and a row of bottles from which he shook out a variety of astringents and hair dressings. He boasted that he could shave a man dry and never nick the skin. With a quid of tobacco in his cheek and a bottle of homemade wine to sip through the day, he talked of dogs and fox hunting and how he told his wife the morning after their wedding night that if she wanted to make the living, she could pick his pants up from the floor and put them on, and he would stay home and cook. She told him, no thanks, you go ahead and wear them. King also claimed that he could remove warts and stop bleeding, secrets he offered to pass along before he died but never did.

Redmond Rose blacksmithed in a shop on Charles Street. Rose could be found there daily, pumping his bellows to bring intense heat to the pit where iron was softened to a white heat. When a farmer needed a piece of odd metal for equipment repair, Rose would mold it out of scrap. He could make a hatchet or shoe a horse. In typical Ap-

Dale Holschuh collection

*Indian Guyan Creek near Scottown at flood stage, 1950. Tobacco and corn crops, ripped from the ground, floated toward Cairo, Illinois.*

palachian good nature, the customer would ask Rose how much he owed. "Oh, whatever you think it was worth," he would reply. The ritual required the buyer to suggest an amount. "How about 50 cents? Is that enough?" and Rose would say, "That's plenty."

Russell Hineman, the village auto mechanic, burrowed under the hood of a 1936 Ford. Signs on the garage wall advertised Willard batteries and reminded customers to *"Keep 'em Flying"* for the U.S. Army Air Corps. Russell tuned the engine, setting the timing, replacing the points and spark plugs. When the Ford's owner got home, a five-minute trip across the big hill, he would brag that his V-8 pulled it in high gear.

Sanford Brumfield, son of a Civil War veteran and new in the grocery business, stocked his glass-top counters with Wings cigarettes, cheap substitutes for the Luckies and Camels that were reserved for American GIs overseas. Dr. Mart's office was closed. Crown City's last doctor had followed the money north. In the graveyard, flowers left on Decoration Day wilted beside the monuments.

Some businesses survived after the war. Among the most successful was Fat Watts's beer joint and grill, on the corner of Gallia Street and the new bypass. Good times, thirsty veterans, and younger boys hardly out of their teens kept Watts's place jumping. By day, WLW in Cincinnati carried Waite Hoyt's play-by-play of Reds games from Crosley Field. By night, the voices of newly popular hillbilly musicians, on records like Merle Travis's *Divorce Me C.O.D.*, spun on the Wurlitzer jukebox. Villages continued to expect that raucous events were likely to occur.

Among the good old boys who frequented Watts's place was Lewis Woodyard, navy veteran and lockmaster on an Ohio River dam. One night in 1947, he was having a few rounds when he got the chance to settle a score. A few weeks earlier, at a bar in Huntington, Oyer Moore had crept up behind Woodyard and struck him in the head with a hammer. Woodyard was left with a steel plate in his head and a bruised ego. Learning that Moore had got up the nerve to come to Crown

City with two of his friends, Woodyard was ready. He gave an account of the incident: "See, when he seen me he started to run and I beat him to the other door, see. I said, 'There ain't no use to run, I got you.' And he jerked a knife out of his jump-jacket pocket. It was opened up. I broke his hand, his wrist right through there [pointing], broke it clear in two, and the knife fell. And he went down and started praying and I just let him have it anyway." Woodyard had hit Moore overhanded with a four-foot-long poker. Moore survived. In 1983 his body was found in a desolate graveyard near Rappsburg in Lawrence County. He had been murdered.

Crown City, however, was starting to mellow. The changing social mores and sophistication that followed WWII were apparent. Business places continued to move over to the new bypass, and Gallia Street, except for a few residences, died. The elementary school closed in 1965, and students were bussed over the hill to the new Hannan Trace Elementary School. Fats Watts sold his last longneck bottle of beer the same year, leaving the village dry for the first time since 1933. The Eagle Rock Tavern, a half-mile north on Route 7, closed in 1988.

A few businesses survive. A barber shop, beauty shop, a gas station, an ice cream and hot dog shop, and a post office are still here. The large grocery and hardware store, located on the old school site, went out of business in 1993. The riverfront is quiet the year around, except when an occasional pleasure boat puts in. When the Hannan Trace High School in Mercerville was consolidated into the River Valley High School 38 miles north at Cheshire, most Crown City parents sent their children into the Fairland District in Lawrence County. About 450 people, retirees and commuters, still live there. The Methodist Church and the Masonic Lodge carry on as usual. And on Old Timers' Day, the last Saturday before Labor Day, gaiety returns as the bands come out, natives visit from distant cities, bluegrass musicians pick and sing, and politicians show up to backslap and shake hands.

# Graveyard

*Goodbye 'til morning comes again*
*The thoughts of death brings grief and pain*
*But could we know how short the night*
*That fades and hides them from our sight*
*Our hearts would sing the glad refrain*
*Goodby 'til morning comes again*

—Author unknown.
This poem was copied from a tombstone
in the Clinch Mountains of Virginia.

Gallia County Historical Society collection

*The Crown City Methodist Church.*

The gravel road turns west from State Route 218 near Crown City in Gallia County, Ohio, and shoots up the side of the hill known as Good Hope. As the road rises it passes an ancient coal bank which nature refuses to reclaim. Honeysuckle vines work hard to swallow a broken beer bottle. Modest oak trees compete with white pines for nourishment from the red clay. Below the road, a rusted barbed-wire fence reveals that a dirt farmer once pastured cattle here. Iron weed grows in profusion in the old meadow. Daisies and wild strawberries, sprinkled with dust from the dry August road, seek rain. From the dark woods that reach down toward the rill that barely trickles now, the rhythm of a bobwhite quail's song drifts down easy.

At the hilltop around the bend, nestled among a dozen giant poplar trees, a white, frame church stands silent in the sunlight. A few feet from the church's front door—as close to heaven as one could get in the early 1800s—the Good Hope graveyard lies. Here, on a great ridge that passes by natural springs, tobacco barns, and dens of copperhead snakes, 500 or more graves hold dead bodies in eternal repose. The first grave was dug in 1828. The most recent, 2001. For 173 years, the dead have come.

> *The leaves of the oak and the willow shall fade,*
> *Be scattered around, and together be laid;*
> *And the young and the old, and the low and the high,*
> *Shall molder to dust and together shall die.***

On the great eastern slope in the warm quiet lies the body of Lafayette Moore, a veteran of the Civil War, and namesake of Frenchman Gilbert du Motier Lafayette who visited the area in 1825. Moore lived from 1842 to 1915. Showing the great sweep of time that brought Guyan Township from the frontier to modern times, his granddaughter is buried a few feet away in the same plot. Colleen Moore, named after a grand siren from the silver screen in the 1920s, lived just 30

**William Knox

days, from July 12 to August 12, 1929. From long dead historic figures to movie stars in 87 years.

No famous people are buried at Good Hope. No great pyramids as those for Egyptian

Author's collection

*Matewan, West Virginia. Families brought food, ate, and made music in summer graveyard gatherings. Author on right.*

Pharaohs; no concrete bunkers such as the one at Springfield where Lincoln is buried; no mausoleums for the rich. No sarcophagi enclose these coffins. The tombstones in this graveyard reflect the lives of plain people. There are veterans here from the Civil War to Vietnam. Their graves are scattered among the others, no rows of crosses as in a military graveyard. The finest stone, ornate granite with floral bas-relief designs and a Masonic logo, marks the grave of James L. Daily (1854 - 1942). His status in life, a landowner, is reflected. Buried here are farmers, drifters, laborers, and the poor. Simple people like Perry Dennison who, at 90, was buried beside the three wives he outlived. He used to brag that his last wife could dig out a groundhog hole as good as any man. Some were suicides, others died in car wrecks. One was crushed in the giant rollers of a grist mill on Indian Guyan Creek. Babies died. Small tombstones with baby lambs sculptured on them set in rows mark tiny graves. Frontier women with names like America and Tennessee lie here. A man named Columbus C. Williams lies near Justin Wells, known for the turtles he used to drag from Williams Creek and carry home in coffee sacks. Felons, drunkards, murderers sleep next to the kind, gentle, and brave. Holy rollers sleep beside skeptics. "We will meet again," "Asleep in Jesus," "Our trust is in God," and "He died as he lived—a Christian," phrases etched in stone testify.

*James Rowe

*The saint who enjoyed the communion of heaven,*
*The sinner who dared to remain unforgiven;*
*The wise and the foolish, the guilty and just,*
*Have quietly mingled their bones in the dust. \**

In the 19th century, few regulations were involved in a burial. Many families set aside small graveyards on family farms. They made their own coffins, prepared the bodies, dug the grave, and read a passage from the Bible in a simple ceremony. As the population increased, and roads improved, local coffin makers set up businesses in villages and towns. These entrepreneurs not only made coffins, they were freelance undertakers and, for a fee, would preach a funeral. Their goods ranged from pine boxes to exotic walnut coffins brushed to a fine finish. One local carpenter made his own coffin, an exquisite baroque model he showed to customers. Family and friends gathered for his funeral, admired the coffin as it went down.

The church that stands by the graveyard evolved soon after the burial ground was laid out. Good Hope Baptist Church was one of

*Caring for and visiting graves of loved ones was a family activity in Appalachia.*

Lavette Compton collection

thousands that were built and nurtured by men and women as they settled into permanent homes on the frontier. True believers felt that religion was the best hope to tame those whiskey-drinking, card-playing, beer joint brawlers, who were always about. Trust in God and prayer provided solace to families in bad times when death was real and frequent. Times were hard. But one could hope for a better home in heaven where, as it was written, the streets were paved with gold. And rugged men with coarse beards and scarred hands sang:

*If I could only hear my mother pray again*
*If I could only hear her tender voice then,*
*So happy I would be*
*It would mean so much to me*
*If I could hear my mother pray again\**

In the 19th century the dead were brought from ceremonies in the home to the church for funeral services. Pine boxes tied down with ropes to wagon beds rolled behind two giant work horses. As

*Before graveyards like Good Hope, people buried the dead in family plots. (Note: Bas relief of clasped hands, words, "Meet Me in Heaven," burial date 1894.)*

Author's collection

* James Rowe

undertakers began to develop skills and government regulations were written, funerals became more elaborate. Undertakers bought fancy hearses which were drawn by black stallions strapped with fine leather harnesses. They led each dark procession to Good Hope time after time, both undertaker and preacher dressed in black finery. Time passed, and in the 1920s, gasoline-powered hearses with custom bodies bolted to frames made by Ford, Packard, Pierce Arrow, and LaSalle came to the hills of Guyan Township.

Inside the church, men and women fanned, blessed the undertaker, and prayed for the dead. Outside, drifters and day laborers in dirty shirts and ties paced and smoked. In the graveyard, an open grave, smooth yellow dirt sides running down to a watery bottom, was ready. Dirt from the grave was covered with artificial grass. Grave diggers set up folding chairs for the family to sit on as the preacher returned the dead to the earth. The sun drifted down toward the horizon. The flowers on the grave wilted. Bystanders trampled the grass near the grave. A whippoorwill hidden in the Berry Road hollow sang as the crowd and family scattered into the dusk.

> *They died, aye they died and the things that are now,*
> *Who walk on the turf that lies over the brow,*
> *Who make in their dwelling a transient abode,*
> *Meet the things that they met on their pilgrimage road.* **

**William Knox

# The Way We Laughed

I was sitting in a beer joint called the Blue Moon in Wellsville, a little town on the Ohio River near Chester, where State Route 7 begins its long journey south and then west. Wellsville's claim to fame is that in 1934, lawmen there gunned down Pretty Boy Floyd, a gangster who had spent his career terrorizing the Midwest. It also claims Bevo Francis, one of the great basketball players of the 1950s, as a native son. There were maybe half a dozen people in the Blue Moon, including the barmaid. Looking up, I couldn't help but take note of a scraggly-looking man trying to enter the place while carrying a door. It was either a door someone had tossed out or one which the man had torn from an old building. When the barmaid saw him, she yelled, "Don't bring that damn door in here." So the man just leaned the door against the outside wall, came in and ordered a beer. He knocked down his beer, walked out, picked up his door and headed on up Main Street.

This is the kind of humor I have seen and heard many times while growing up in Appalachia. Short. Sharp. Irreverent. Deadpan. Hard times, death, poverty, and a general melancholy among the people would at times give way to irony. The humor I saw and heard was delivered with nuances, inflections, and nonverbal expressions impossible to convert to mere printed words. Not long, drawn-out tales or allegories. Not parables or epiphanies. Simple and spare, spur-of-the-moment comments and behaviors. Some, however, live on through the years as oral tradition. During World War II, President Franklin Roosevelt appealed to all to give or sell scrap iron and aluminum for the war effort. While playing in the barn near my childhood home in

*Family and friends enjoy watermelons fresh from the fields in Waterloo, Ohio, circa 1900.*

Crown City, Ohio, I pointed out to my young Republican playmate two nice scrap aluminum coffee pots. Freddie replied, alluding to the president in a snotty way, "Rosie ain't going to get that." Every time we saw a piece of scrap after that, someone would say, "Are you sure you want to give that to Rosie?"

Landowners in their roles as bosses often deviled day laborers and drifters. They dished out a kind of mental torment, or, as us city folks say, a Mel Torme, to people who were seen as harmless, unable to stand up against authority figures. One of my uncles greeted a hired hand, well into his fifties, with at least 13 children among three wives looking for his 14th child: "James, you're going to have to lock your door when you leave the house, some man's slipping in over there when you're out." This came from a deacon in the church who said he would not take a drink even if his life were threatened. James did have sense enough to look sideways.

Few were exempt from the depreciation of others and self. If a teacher picked up a nickname like Squirt or Hog Face, it was his for life. The teachers and others I knew did not seem to understand that if they had laughed at themselves and adopted the tag they would have taken the power from it. But these putdowns were always out for everyone to see on the restroom walls. One Arms, One Lungs, along with a variety of Slims, Big Mouths, No Necks, Big Foots, Corn Breads, and Weasels were common nicknames among the hills and hollows of Gallia and Lawrence Counties in southern Ohio. These names were given with a good feeling and received by their owners with humor and acceptance. You still see these in obituaries in Appalachia. It may be a class thing. Death notices for higher-educated and rich people seldom have a nickname listed in their death notices. A lady named Cricket is more likely to work at the bowling alley than as a medical doctor.

We laughed about the school teacher whose high heels slipped on the terrazzo, throwing her on her butt and tossing an overhead projector into the air. A lady, taking her first car ride, jumped out of an open-top car into brush as she and the driver topped a hill. Aunt Bessie

*DeHaven's Ice Cream Parlor, Ironton, Ohio, circa 1940. You would smile, too, if you could get three dips of ice cream for a nickel. Saturdays were trading days when farmers went to town to sell products and animals, buy hardware and other things they could not get in local stores. Saturday in town was also a time for socializing. The streets were crowded with folks gossiping and talking politics.*

McKinley always told that particular story with much laughter. Aunt Bessie and her husband were marvelous truck farmers. A good truck farmer goes to market early while the buyers still have money. Another trader, going with my uncle to market one summer morning, drove into the driveway at 1:30 a.m. My uncle greeted him, "Come on in and have some breakfast. I've already had mine."

Most people treasured the virtues of truth and honesty. Knowing you would see these same people all your life made for good social discipline. However, there were elements of acceptable goofiness and rascality. One of my aunts, packing tomatoes in peck baskets for market, would slip little toads and harmless spiders into the sealed containers. An uncle, making a deal for a new Chevrolet, took his trade-in to the dealer with a dead skunk in the trunk. A friend, perturbed at losing some coins in a newspaper vending machine, came back on other days and slipped a neat copy of an outdated paper on top of the stack. When my brother and I were young, our dad ordered a hat in the mail. It was one of those wide-brimmed hats like Crocodile Dundee wears; dark brown, it would have been right at home in Montana. For some reason, he put it in the deep freezer along with two or three hundred pounds of deer meat and a couple of muskrats dad had trapped before the season came in. My brother came to me and said he thought Dad was going crazy, because he had put his hat in the freezer. Apparently, this was a hat that had to be cured. Now my Dad was a small man with a small head. When he put this hat on he looked like the character in Dick Tracy years ago called the Hat. His hat was his head. Tracy cornered him after a few weeks and his words were: "Hat, you rat." We all had a good laugh when Dad showed up with this hat on and, in a few days, he was at the kitchen table wrapping it up to send back.

We used to name our farm animals after people we knew. We had a chicken who looked like Webster Newton, a cow who looked like Harold Murray. People wore odd clothes. We had a teacher who was a veteran of World War II and who had his Army uniforms dyed ma-

Lois Eanes collection

*Walter Eanes, Brenda Jude, Matewan, West Virginia, circa 1950.*

roon and wore them to work. Teachers would wear the same greasy tie every day for a month complemented by double-knit pants and wingtips. My dad had some heavy wool plaid shirts he finally gave away to some poor man who worked for us. In the heat of August, taking in hay, he would have on one of these shirts. Shirts that would burn you up in the dead of winter. We laughed to survive. There were always hucksters coming along selling stuff. In the heart of the depression we bought lightning rods for the house. They were pretty, but what was the chance a house would be struck? A kitchenware salesman sold my mother some dishes. In his pitch he threw a plate against a wall to show they were unbreakable. Within a few weeks, she found out that if she dropped a plate it broke into a hundred pieces.

Most people would not lie about a horse's age or defects. But if you could skin somebody by buying cheap and selling high, it was something to laugh about. If you could trade the Raleigh man an overripe watermelon for a jar of salve, it was not thought of as something you needed to testify about at church. My friends and I went joyriding one summer night in an old Model T Ford whose noise on starting

*Celeste Pierce plays at the Big Laurel Mountain School, Marrowbone, West Virginia, circa 1985.*

would wake the dead. We fired it up and drove it four or five miles, over the hill to Platform, then to Crown City, back over the Miller hill and home. The owner, if he ever knew it, never let on. My oldest brother sold his Model T Ford to a friend, took the money, hitchhiked to town and bought a pair of brown and white wingtips. He spent the summer sporting his way to church and pie suppers on foot. A relative from an older generation rolled his old car over into Indian Guyan Creek. As soon as someone found him, another person went to tell his mother that Clarence had had a wreck. When a neighbor finally got Clarence out and, soaked with water, oil, and gasoline, took him home he said, "Here's Clarence, he's all right." His mother, typical of the Appalachian mothers to whom worry and melancholia were mind sets, said, "That's not Clarence, he got killed in a car wreck". When I got hold of a little money, I bought myself a used Buick Roadmaster convertible. Got it from Sheline Motors. There was always one good car on his lot in Gallipolis. But if you started to look at it he would say, "I'm sorry, that's my personal car." When I was showing the Buick around one of my friends said, "Hey, it's got that damned leather upholstering." When my family saw me riding through town in December with the top down, they ducked into the nearest store with that look of, "He ain't nobody I know," on their faces.

My mother kept family pictures in old shoe boxes. They were never in order, you would find everything from last summer's picture of someone holding up a six-foot-long blacksnake to pictures from the 19th century of old men and women in high collars and velvet dresses. They were funny. My older sister always cut her image out of the pictures leaving the other persons in the picture intact. Mom would say, "That's your sister, isn't her dress cute." Everyone was subject to be made fun of because they usually looked stupid. We looked to see who was the skinniest, the fattest, ones with big noses. There was a family in the community who always took pictures of one another in front of the outhouse. Cars were the most common backdrop, old rattle traps with fenders hanging, the Burger Beer logo gleaming from the spare tire cover that hung on the trunk. You would see men in their Sunday best, hat cocked to one side, a cigarette dangling from their lips. Children dressed up for church, for some reason, always frowning or scowling. We had pic-

Paula Newsome collection

*Marrowbone Creek, West Virginia, circa 1940. Don't like the way you look in a picture?* Tear out your face.

tures no one in the family could identify. For all we knew they were not even family, just pictures of long-lost or long-dead folks we didn't want to throw away; they were too funny. We had pictures of everything: pets, cows, pigs, barns, floods, fallen trees, wheelbarrows, plows, dead animals brought in from the hunt. One of my uncles gave us a picture taken by a professional photographer that showed him holding his shotgun, proud as Ernest Hemingway over a dead lion, surrounded by at least three hundred dead crows.

# White Whiskey

The trees along the Tennessee highland ridges were dark, and their limbs arched out over the open flats. The shadows formed by the westward sun as it dropped down toward the horizon were long and jagged. At the head of the hollows, sweet limestone water seeped from the rocks and trickled along zigzag paths on its trip to the rivulets below. As the water slipped down, pools were formed around the rusted metal parts of abandoned moonshine stills. In the sparse areas that had been grubbed out, green plants with slender ribbed leaves blossomed as the deep summer heat coaxed the sap down. The marijuana crop that grew tough beyond the redbrush was strong and green. And the high

*Kentucky moonshine still and moonshiners, circa 1925.*

sheriff's men had, so far, passed it by. But this is a story that began 250 years ago, 3,000 miles eastward in the Irish Republic of Ulster.

Rows of sheep and their herdsmen walked along the banks of the moors in the valleys of the Sperrin Mountains. Southward, the Glenelly River, salmon running in its cold, shallow water, rushed toward the North Atlantic. In the villages of Armagh, Londonderry, and Ballygawley, rugged men in wool tweeds gathered in public houses to toast their families and curse the Stuart King. This was the Irish Province of Ulster in the early eighteenth century. Historians believe that it was in this region as early as 1490 that men first developed the art of producing grain whiskey.

The residents of Ulster were, primarily, descendants of the tall, blue-eyed Celts who came to Ireland from central Europe before the birth of Christ. Down through the years, the territory was invaded and colonized by the Norsemen, Normans, English, and Scots. But during the reign of King James I in the 17th century, with both Scotland and Ireland under his domain, thousands of Scottish Protestants were invited to immigrate to the province of Ulster. In an attempt to balance off the Catholic north and populate the Ulster lowlands, James promised them a deal: They could choose where they lived, own guns, worship freely, and make untaxed whiskey. By the middle of the 17th century, Ulster had assimilated the newcomers and the evolution of the Scotch Irish began. Together, they drained marshy bogs, cultivated potatoes, and developed the linen and woolen industries. But when they combined their legendary knowledge of whiskey making, they struck a lasting bond and produced a product that would affect the culture of the world thereafter. The clean, white whiskey they distilled among the glens of Ulster was the forerunner of Appalachian moonshine and, later, Kentucky bourbon.

The destiny of the citizens of Northern Ireland continued to be one of dissent to the annoyances of their central government. Badgered by excise taxes on whiskey and deadly famines, however painful it was for them to leave their families and native land, they looked westward in their quest for freedom. In America, the Pennsylvania colony under the leadership of William Penn promised a respite from their unrest. Penn's tolerance for religions and his commitment to democratic ideals appealed to the Ulstermen. And from 1717 to 1776 at least 400,000 Scotch-Irish settlers became American immigrants. Their personal effects were few, but their love for independence and their ability to make whiskey came with them to the hills of western Pennsylvania.

The Scotch-Irish, along with other immigrants, came to a land of unparalleled resources. The forests of the Allegheny Mountains, the rivers, the fish and game, the growing cities, and an unlimited frontier lay before them. They were, moreover, thirsty for a wide variety of distilled and fermented spirits which had flowed freely in the colonies for at least a hundred years. The ancient social customs of England and other European countries were entrenched. The Pilgrims brought a cache of liquor with them on the Mayflower. The ship that carried Governor John Winthrop to the Massachusetts Bay Colony also carried 42 tons of beer. Early in the 17th century the Virginia Assembly asked newcomers to bring enough liquor with them to drink until they could make the transition to Virginia water. An Episcopalian minister, George Thorpe, operated a crude distillery on the banks of the James River. A few miles west in Pennsylvania, William Penn operated a brewery on his estate. Many Colonists were so proud of their distilling efforts that they pitched the fact to Europeans to help entice them to settle in America. A few years later, George Washington operated a still at his Dogue farm near Mount Vernon.

Many other revered names in American history were associated with taverns in their home towns. Paul Revere and Sam Adams loafed at the Green Dragon in Boston. Patrick Henry tended bar in a tavern at Hanover. The Sons of Liberty held court at the Burns Coffee House near Trinity Church in New York. And it was at John Buckman's tavern in Lexington, Massachusetts, that the Minutemen assembled before they took up their charge against the Crown's men.

Although corn and barley were used as a base for the distillation of liquor in scattered areas, most of the early spirits were made from the fruits that grew wild in the unspoiled wilderness and from the orchards that were a staple of rural life. And when the New England shipowners began to bring molasses home with them from their West Indies slave trading runs, rum soon became the drink of choice among the Colonists.

The churches and the taverns were complementary institutions in early America. With the use of liquor almost universal and the support of the Scriptures' admonition to "...drink thy wine with a merry heart..." drinks were available at most social occasions. Funerals, contract signings, political rallies, weddings, ordinations, criminal trials, and log rollings were typical events where liquor was part of the ceremonies. Churches and taverns were built close together so that worshipers at the all-day church ordeals could seek respite at noon in the warmth of the tavern where an open fireplace contrasted the coldness of the sanctuaries. By 1720 these social functions and the medicinal use of liquors included the consumption of 12,000 gallons of rum in one year. Only a few reservations were drawn by Increase Mather and his brother Cotton, and their concerns were that the poor and lower classes would spend their meager incomes on booze and that their fellow clergymen might set poor examples.

As the distillation and drinking of spirits continued unabated, minor rumblings in support of abstinence were being advanced by selected leaders among the Methodist denomination. And in local communities and provinces as distant as the Virginia colony, liquor regulation and excise taxes were introduced in the various assemblies. But it was in southwest Pennsylvania with its high concentration of Scotch-Irish settlers that the largest number of distilleries operated. With the young nation 21 million dollars in debt from the Revolutionary War and with the Federalist, Alexander Hamilton, at the helm of the Federal Treasury, it was inevitable that a Federal excise tax on whiskey was proposed. With the support of President George Washington and the Congress agreeing, in 1791, a tax on whiskey was imposed; and rewards were offered to spies for reporting on their neighbors. Once again, as the settlers had been accustomed to in their native Ireland, they were faced with what they perceived as governmental tyranny, an anathema to them. With grain the main cash crop of the mountain farmers and with its distillation into whiskey the only profitable way to market it, it was no wonder that hordes of angry farmers oiled up their squirrel guns. And so the Whiskey Boys—antifederalist, anti-tax, and anti-Indian—assembled. In October 1794, 5,000 strong, they advanced toward Pittsburgh on the banks of the Monongahela River. At the urging of President Washington, the governors of Maryland, Virginia, Pennsylvania, and New Jersey drafted an army of 13,000 men. President George Washington personally reviewed the troops and Commander Henry "Lighthorse Harry" Lee marched the troops to the outskirts of Pittsburgh. When the Federal troops arrived, the loosely organized uprising was already in disarray. With their point made, they went forward raiding chicken coops and drinking large quantities of the product at the heart of the problem.

The Whiskey Rebellion established the young central government as a force to be leery of. It also inspired the Scotch-Irish to move on. And with their families and meager belongings, which usually included a copper still, a worm, a proof vial, and a mash stick, they took the Great Philadelphia Wagon Road down through the Blue Ridge Mountains. Some traveled farther into the highlands across the Wilderness Road into Kentucky and Tennessee, through the Cumberland Gap toward the Ohio River. Others moved into the western North and South Carolina, and northern Georgia. And it was in these remote mountains and plateaus that the American moonshiner took hold and developed a subculture that captured the interest of historians, sociologists, novelists, and social reformers.

As the Scotch-Irish settlers penetrated the Appalachian highlands and joined the small band of English and French Huguenot pioneers already there, their future held new promise. The repeal of the Federal spirit tax in 1802 and the settlers' assimilation into the social, economic, political, and geographic elements of the highlands were factors which helped their culture flourish. The quick branches that tumbled down into the hollows provided water and small fish. Natural springs, many of them with limestone water, complemented the still sites. The broad escarpments were fertile with wild mountain laurel, bluebells, chicory, and bloodroot. After grubbing, hillside flats were turned into cornfields. Ginseng, wintergreen, elderberries, blackberries, and raspberries grew profusely along the damp ravines. Hickory, locust, red cedar, white pine, black walnut, maple and oak trees extended the mountains upward and sheltered the living things below. Bobwhite quail, killdeers, horned owls, ruffed grouse, crows, passenger pigeons, and wild turkeys made the primeval forests their natural habitat. Foxes, whitetail deer, squirrels, bears, weasels, and bobcats roamed the vast area. And in the hollows, rich bottom land was black and fertile; creeks and rivers teemed with fish and fur-bearing animals.

But the land was untamed, sometimes vicious. Timber rattlers and copperheads snuggled beneath the limestone rocks. Indians still held tenaciously to selected areas in the wilderness. The winters were cold, shelter was scarce, and medical doctors were hard to find. Roads were no more than traces wide enough for a horse and wagon or a yoke of oxen. Communication with the settlements in the east was difficult and with the west, impossible. Recreation was often no more than cultivating a wild flower or waiting for a groundhog to come out of a hole.

These pioneers were, however, people of tough spirit and bold character. They settled in, grubbed the flats, and gave names to places such as Turkey Creek, Greasy Ridge, Devil's Jump, Little Bullskin, and Hazard. They were so physically and spiritually congruent with the land that, chameleon like, they blended with the environment. Sociologists have advanced a number of reasons why they settled in a harsh and hilly land where only the most industrious could survive rather than move on to the western prairies as many other pioneers did. Some believe that, since their ancestors lived in the tough environments of Scotland and Ireland, they were genetically adapted to Appalachia. Others believe that the highlands made them what they were, that children born in the mountains soaked up the environment and melded naturally to the hills. Still others believe their character demanded isolation, community scared them, and their mistrust of government added to the way they cherished their respite from the middle class. There is probably some truth in all of these ideas. However, none of them is totally satisfactory. There was community—not the kind that organized social bodies like the Grange, but more a family type of cleverness or, perhaps, a clannishness that transcended phony rituals and incantations. The main reason they established homes in the mountains and raised families that extended into several generations was that children were reluctant to leave the aid and succor of the old folks at home or even the old shepherd dog that slept on the porch. Beyond the hills was land unknown, a land that, to them, lacked community. In the hills there was camaraderie and family. Work and play were team efforts by necessity. Hogs were butchered, corn shucked, foot logs lifted and placed, and barns raised by groups of young and old, male and female together. They stayed on and developed the Appalachian culture for noble reasons.

And they made and sold moonshine whiskey. Why not? Corn was easy to grow on the hillside flats and, turned into whiskey, was easy to transport and to store. Moral admonitions emerging from the Methodist preachers and the Anti-Saloon League were ignored in the highlands. Whiskey could be traded for goods or sold for cash. For a government to attempt to control what one grew on one's own land was undemocratic at best. Whiskey was badly needed for medicine and recreation. It was not easy for the mountaineer to understand why it was wrong for him to operate a hundred-gallon still while it was legal for large distilleries to produce and sell the same product. The drink they made in these early years, pure and white, sometimes aged a month or two in wooden barrels, was a product made with pride. Had it been legal, and had the mountaineer been one to engage in such folderol, moonshine whiskey samples would have been put into competition at the county fairs along with canned green beans and stalks of tobacco.

The repeal of the second Federal tax on whiskey in 1817 that was in effect for three years to help pay for the War of 1812 and the extension of the frontier beyond the Allegheny Mountains westward created a wide-open market for distilled spirits. Complementing the moonshiners in the hills, numerous whiskey makers plied their craft legally in the more prosperous open regions in Kentucky and Tennessee. Distillation methods advanced. Copper condensing chambers, the use of steam to raise the temperature of the mash to vaporization without scorching, and the process of a second distillation called doubling were developed during this period. James C. Crow, a Scotch-Irish descendent, developed the sour mash process and introduced the saccharometer, the thermometer, the hydrometer, and sanitation procedures to the craft. Two-year-old or "aged" whiskey was advertised. When the whiskey was siphoned off later, its color was red, and Kentucky bourbon, an aromatic, smoother whiskey purged of impurities, was born. The Marquis de Lafayette, visiting from France, enjoyed shots of it at Ashland, Kentucky, in 1824.

Whiskey continued to be a medium of exchange. It was used as barter for goods from the Indians, sold from spigot barrels in general stores, traded for stud fees, and communities grew in places where the still house was the leading industry. In 1819, with whiskey selling for about a quarter per gallon, 2 million gallons were shipped down the Mississippi to the port of New Orleans from Tennessee, Kentucky, Ohio, and Indiana. Thomas Lincoln, young Abraham in tow, carried ten barrels of whiskey which he received as partial payment for his farm with him to Indiana in 1816. A few years later, the young Abraham sold it himself at the Lincoln-Berry store in New Salem, Illinois. John James Audubon took 300 barrels full with him when he left his store and family in Henderson, Kentucky, and headed for Missouri to sketch birds. Gold seekers, sod busters, hide hunters, note shavers, trappers, mule skinners, and bull whackers went west with pints of white whiskey in their saddle bags.

But as communities developed and settlements became permanent, voices of dissent arose. Dr. Benjamin Rush, a Pennsylvania doctor, declared after the Revolutionary War that soldiers didn't need whiskey, that it might even be harmful. President James Monroe ordered whiskey removed from Army rations. By 1820, Kentucky and other selected states began to regulate tippling houses. Preachers through the Midwest and in parts of Appalachia, in a wave of Victorian righteousness, flailed away at the whiskey makers. Along with learning, jewelry, and pride, the manufacture and use of whiskey were declared sins. Societies such as the Anti-Saloon League, the Prohibition Party, the Women's Christian Temperance Union, and the National Temperance Society were formed during the nineteenth century to counteract what they saw as the down side of drinking. And once again the Federal Government joined the cause. In 1862 the Internal Revenue Service was established and whiskey was taxed at 20 cents per gallon. The prohibitionists lashed out against the proliferation of saloons in the urban Midwest and the fact that Kentucky exported more whiskey than flour. Supported by Eastern industrialists who knew they couldn't sell hardware to settlers who had spent what little cash they had on whiskey, and led by the fire-breathing Carrie Nation, they fanned out across the land. They argued their cause on the lyceum circuit and used parlor tricks, ghastly charts, and pledge cards to entice their audiences. They believed that any drinking was in excess and that moderation was unacceptable. Methodist ministers prayed to God that any ground where crops suitable for whiskey-making grew might become fallow. Prohibition became the rallying point for a variety of social forces. The issue was seen as a struggle between virtuous, God-fearing rural elements and pleasure-seeking, cultivated urban dwellers.

The 19th century, with all its progress and rascality, had little ef-

fect on the Appalachian highlanders. They were well aware of the Civil
War, because large numbers of them, even in states as far south as
Tennessee, fought for the Union. They were Republican minorities in
Democratic areas who had no identification with the South's defiant
attitude toward slavery. And by their nature, the branch water mountaineers up the creeks and on the hog back ridges maintained their
political and social independence. Their ethics and their personal effects remained utilitarian. Gentle and loving with children, they
might, however, kill a neighbor over a line fence dispute. So in spite
of Federal laws, revenue agents, and the rising tide of prohibition, the
highlanders stocked up on one-quart mason jars and sugar and continued to turn corn into drink. In 1876 the IRS reported that the mountains contained at least 3,000 illegal stills capable of producing up to
50 gallons of white whiskey daily. Federal seizures of stills averaged
1,000 per year. An IRS report in 1880 listed 4,061 stills seized, 7,339
persons arrested, 26 officers killed, and 56 wounded. Even the mighty
Lt. Col. George Custer took Federal troops into Kentucky in 1871 in a
futile attempt to intimidate the illegal distillers. As the 20th century
broke through, newspapers, magazines, and books began to report
events of both fact and imagination about the Appalachian highlanders. Authors described them as banditti and outlaws trapped in a social system they could not control, living in a past past marked by
violence and anarchic individualism. A romantic aura developed
around its illegality. Seen by outsiders as a peculiar land of heroism,
self-sacrifice, and hard work, Appalachia became a land to itself; a
place where time stood still. And it was from the writings in popular
magazines and fiction that the archetype mountaineer was drawn:
an ignorant hillbilly who wore bib overalls, drank whiskey from jugs,
and lived on corn bread and beans. But with whiskey selling for three
dollars a gallon, life in the highlands went on as usual. Every belling,
coon hunt, bee tree cutting, field trial, and music festival was ritual-
ized with the renowned liquor. Smuggled out in devious ways such as
hiding it under the top layer of peaches in baskets, moonshine was

available from bellhops in city hotels or down at the livery stable. Even while Wayne B. Wheeler was directing the Anti-Saloon League from his office in Columbus, Ohio, the mountaineer was more concerned with proofing whiskey by the size and duration of the bead at the top of the jar: at 85 proof where the bead hung on top soon to flash off; at 100 proof, called a good shake; or at 160 proof, which was 80 percent alcohol with beads standing on the surface of the whiskey. They called this horse eyes.

By the time Woodrow Wilson became president, the goal of the Prohibitionists to outlaw drinking in America had become a national obsession. The pioneer tradition of hard drinking, the skid row atmosphere of the saloon, the anti-German feelings during World War I, the belief that sober soldiers fought better, the need for more grain to produce bread, and the naive quest for everlasting peace and Utopia became concepts that the wets and moderates could not counteract. Evangelist Billy Sunday preached for the drys in massive tent meetings across the land. Scholars rewrote the Bible, substituting the word "juice" for "wine." Moralists argued that gin and applejack, a cheap drink fondly called strip-and-go-naked, must be kept from blacks and poor people. So a movement that had begun in the Methodist church in 1840 reached its zenith in 1919. Following the actions of legislatures in the states of Georgia, North Carolina, Tennessee, Mississippi, West Virginia, and Oklahoma, the United States Congress passed the Eighteenth Amendment over President Woodrow Wilson's veto. On January 17, 1920, the door on legal drinking was slammed shut throughout the United States. Fredrick Allen wrote that "...the country accepted it not only willingly, but almost absent-mindedly." A spokesman for the Anti-Saloon League proclaimed that an era of "...clear thinking and clean living..." was at hand. And Federal Commissioner John Kramer warned that "...this law will be obeyed in cities, large and small." The great saloons of the cities with their gilt beer signs, swinging doors, brass rails, back bar mirrors, and racy paintings such as "Saturday Night" and "Venus at the Bath" were bolted and locked. These egalitarian institutions whose staples were cold beer and red whiskey and their bartenders in long-sleeve shirts and slicked down hair, Sweet Caporal cigarettes hanging from their lips, closed up. When prohibition ended, they were reopened as tap rooms, cocktail lounges, cafes, places, piano bars, beer gardens, bars, grilles, and beer joints. On that cold night when prohibition came down, Billy Sunday's congregation may have sung, "Bringing in the Sheaves," but in the hollows of Cocke County, Tennessee, the muffled sounds of thumper kegs attached to pot stills drifted unfettered across the valleys.

The Appalachian mountaineers, typically unaffected by social and political events beyond the hills, discovered that the Eighteenth Amendment penetrated even the most remote geographic regions. In 1920, the moonshine that had retailed for two dollars a gallon was suddenly worth $22. This increase in demand and the potential for profit, heretofore unknown to moonshiners, was warmly accepted by those who succumbed to greed. Many of the craftsmen, who once took pride in clean corn whiskey, degenerated into unscrupulous profiteers. Sugar was substituted for grain meal, fermentation was enhanced by adding carbide, volume was increased by cutting the moonshine with water, glycerine, food coloring, formaldehyde, and wood alcohol. In one three-day period in 1920, 23 men were killed by drinking moonshine that contained wood alcohol. Many others were blinded or paralyzed. Prohibition officials themselves, moreover, deliberately poisoned industrial alcohol with mercury, pyridine, iodine, and sulfuric acid.

Attempts at enforcement of prohibition laws drove the moonshiners further back into the woods. Neighbors fought neighbors as the revenue officers sought out stool pigeons. Local and federal agents entered into collusion and payoffs with moonshiners. Confiscated moonshine was sometimes stolen and drunk by the agents themselves. Mountain moonshining became big business. Two years into prohibition, the government reported 54,000 stills raided

*Glen Holschuh's grocery, Scottown, Ohio, circa 1950. Storekeepers became suspicious when patrons asked for sugar in 100-pound sacks.*

and 83,000 persons arrested. With 400 million gallons of moonshine transported annually out of Appalachia for urban consumption, hijackings of the goods in transit compounded an already difficult problem. The reliable corn whiskey that helped quench the thirst of the pioneers in the westward expansion had, overnight, become white lightning, coffin varnish, sheep dip, horse liniment, panther piss, and rotgut.

The social and political effects of prohibition outside Appalachia were even more dramatic. The concept of illegal drinking clashed with other social phenomena. The prosperity following World War I, the availability of automobile and highway expansion, the mass market for radios and other luxury goods, the increase in educational opportunities, and women's suffrage complemented an era that became mad, noisy, lawless, and affluent. Hip flasks became status symbols, women in rouge and short skirts were attracted to the speakeasies, and tailor-made cigarettes became fashionable. Personalities such as

Peaches Browning, Gertrude Ederle, Charles Lindbergh, Elliot Ness, Al Capone, Dutch Shultz, Rudolph Valentino, Rudy Vallee, and Aimee Simple McPherson captivated a nation hungry for a good time.

This was prohibition. Perjurers, embezzlers, bootleggers, spies, informers, and liars, a country caught up in larceny. But as the nation danced all night to the shuffle and the slow drag, the stock market collapse of 1929 left bewilderment and chaos. It was inevitable, then, that the administration of Franklin Roosevelt would succeed in ratification of the twenty-first amendment. In December 1933, the country returned to local option regarding the sale and use of legal alcohol. In Appalachia, however, just as sure as the killdeer's song from the deep wood, the moonshine

Lois Eanes collection

*Howard and Ethel Booth, Matewan, West Virginia, during the roaring twenties.*

business went on. The return of legal liquor to much of the United States did result in a decrease in moonshine production. With the tax on whiskey down to two dollars per gallon in 1933, still seizures dropped to 16,465, 30% fewer than the first year of prohibition. New roads and more automobiles, the inability of the legal liquor industry to recoup and supply the demand, and the economic depression of the 1930s were, however, among the causes of the revitalization of moonshining. By 1935, Franklin County, Virginia, had become the wettest section in the United States. In a massive federal trial there, several local merchants, auto salesmen, financiers, sheriffs, deputies, members of the state prohibition forces, federal revenue men, and moonshiners were found guilty of a variety of crimes involving the production and bootlegging of illicit whiskey. Carter Lee, a grand nephew of Robert E. Lee, was among those indicted. In the four-year period from 1935 to 1939, an estimated 3,500,000 gallons of moonshine was shipped out of Franklin County. But still seizures continued to decline with 11,407 reported in 1938.

In the late thirties and early forties, the use of automobiles to transport moonshine by night at high speed out of the Appalachian highlands become the most dramatic dimension in the industry. Among the cars used by the trippers, the 1940 Ford coupe was the most reliable. With the back seat and trunk converted into a 250-gallon tank, and the engine souped up with superchargers, multiple carburetors, override springs and Columbia rear ends, these sleek vehicles, driven by a new generation of moonshine operators, brought the industry into the 20th century. Night after night they burnt up the crooked roads that led out of Dawson County, Georgia; Cocke County, Tennessee; and Wilkes County, North Carolina, the three largest moonshining areas in the early 1940s. Speeding up to 125 miles an hour, throwing out nails and smoke behind them, pulling off U-turns at high speed, and darting across fields to evade police cars in chase, they pulled their loads into Knoxville, Atlanta, Asheville, and Greenville to bootleggers who waited for them in hidden warehouses. Master drivers, they perfected the execution of fast curves by using full acceleration as the car broke adhesion from the roadway and slid sideways through the turns.

When the police got faster cars, the trippers switched to Offenhauser engines. Dressed in business suits and white shirts with plastic pencil holders in their pockets, they moved 50,000 gallons of whiskey into Atlanta in 1940. The most famous of the early trippers,

Lloyd Seay, of Dawsonville, Georgia, even transferred his driving skills to stock car racing. After winning a Sunday afternoon race at the Lakewood Speedway in 1941, he was killed in a fight with a cousin over a load of sugar. His tombstone features a bas relief of his 1940 Ford with his picture in the driver's seat. The nature of the moonshiner, however, continued to be presented as a person of gentle spirits caught in a vicious environment. After visiting the Cocke County, Tennessee, area, newspaper columnist Ernie Pyle wrote that the mountaineers gave him a new idea of honor. Amazed by the friendship they displayed toward those who helped prosecute them, and wondering how else they could make a living, he proclaimed that they were anything but criminals. World War II and the social upheaval that went along with it had a big effect on the Appalachian mountaineer. Most of the able, young men went off to military service. Soon the provincial lads from remote regions like Mingo County, West Virginia, were carousing away the evening in distant cities while Elton Britt's version of *There's A Star Spangled Banner Waving Somewhere* blasted from the jukeboxes. Sugar was rationed, and copper was almost impossible to hold onto as President Franklin Roosevelt called for patriotic citizens to give their scrap metal to the war effort. With many of the moonshine customers away, still seizures in 1943 dropped to the lowest since 1918 with 5,654 reported by the Alcohol, Tobacco, and Firearms Division of the IRS. Moreover, the tax had risen to six dollars per gallon. When the boys returned after the war, Appalachia was still the same. But they were different. They found good times and a regular payday, saw young women working at jobs in factories for cash money, and had learned about a lively world and opportunities elsewhere. Thousands of Appalachians left the area for good. Painful as it was to break with family tradition and settle outside the clan, they went north in droves where the post-war prosperity in the heavy industries of Akron, Detroit, and Chicago welcomed them among the amalgamation of earlier immigrants. Even many of those who chose not to move away left the hillside cabins, their mothers' nurture, and the family graveyards, going off to colleges on the GI Bill. But just when the authorities thought moonshining was on the way out, a recession in the South, an increase in the whiskey tax to $10.50 per gallon, the return home from the North of many of those who had gone there to settle, and the Korean War brought about yet another resurgence of moonshining. In the mid-fifties the three major centers for moonshine production—Dawson County, Georgia; Cocke County, Tennessee; and Wilkes County, North Carolina—were back in production. Backed up by smaller pockets of activity in Greene County, Tennessee; the Big Bend region of Georgia; Dark Corner, South Carolina; Golden Pond, Kentucky; Franklin County, Virginia; eastern Kentucky; southern West Virginia; and southern Ohio, production and sales approached the 1935 level. In the month of September 1955, 1,261 stills were seized in the United States. The Cincinnati and Atlanta Bureaus of the ATF counted 1,184 of these seizures in their geographic jurisdiction. Total seizures for the year amounted to 12,509.

After 1955, moonshine production tapered off. Improvement in communications, education, mobility, and economics finally made a significant impact on the lives of the Appalachian highlanders. Interstate highways crisscrossed the mountains and valleys, satellite dishes and cables brought television and the world into the remote cabins, jobs became easier to get in Hickory, North Carolina, than in Akron, Ohio, and school improvements helped to create more legitimate opportunities for the residents of the Appalachian South. The social change was so great that during the 1980s many working-age people moved from the rust-besieged cities of the North to more prosperous areas of southern Appalachia. In 1975, still seizures by federal agents dropped to 889 and by 1987, three. The great moonshine era had passed. But it wasn't dead.

As the 20th century breaks loose, much of Appalachia still lacks jobs and good schools. With the government men working on too many guns and weed, moonshiners have popped up again. In Rocky Mount, Virginia, the hub of today's trade, making whiskey is on the rise. Makers here have stills that hold 800 gallons or more. Escaping taxes, they clear nine dollars a gallon. Using federal money-laundering statutes, the federal agents began Operation Lightning Strike and have confiscated 10,000 gallons of moonshine, supplies of sugar, Mason jars, guns, and scanners. One suspect killed himself.

Although most locals in moonshine areas would prefer to get away from the past, move into newer ways, and see homemade whiskey become a quaint relic of times past, they still defend the heritage. A few orthodontists and college deans in the region add a touch of local lore when drinks are served to out-of-town guests. Moonshine can still be bought, if the seller knows the patron is all right, in some southern roadhouses far back from the Holiday Inns along the interstates where travelers sip wine coolers in hotel lounges. The trippers are gone, replaced by tourists in minivans headed for Dollywood and the Great Smokies. In the backwoods, a few old-timers still run off a batch of moonshine now and then to augment the monthly checks they draw down from the black lung fund or Social Security. And there are still a few bootleggers in the region who will, for a good price, slip a pint of Jim Beam to a friend who wants to save a trip to town and the retail store. In 1998, down at Golden Pond, Kentucky, in The Land Between the Lakes, a retired moonshiner, with the help of a former federal agent, demonstrated the art of making moonshine in a setting resembling a county fair, as children watched in awe.

# Making Melancholia

They made music through the long, smoky nights in beer joints on Parsons Avenue. The kinds of music those of us who grew up in Appalachia in the forties and fifties have lodged in our souls. Crisp arpeggios run on guitars always bouncing to the rhythm of the thumb picked G string. Minor riffs evoking an intense melancholia that even a half dozen cold longnecks would not soothe. Smoke from Camels curling up from their perches on ends of guitar string stubs. Breaks taken by turns at the single microphone by pickers on banjos, mandolins, flattop guitars, upright basses and fiddles. The Green River boys. Five young men lately out of the hollows of Kentucky, Tennessee, West Virginia, and southern Ohio. Workers by day at brawny factories like Jeffrey's Iron. Musicians on Friday and Saturday nights at one of Columbus, Ohio's hillbilly hangouts called Dave's Place. Between sets at this regular gig, they joined in

Jo Ann Null collection

*Bluegrass band from West Virginia, players unidentified.*

with friends and wives, listening to the jukebox, talking about rebuilt carburetors, and the driving time to Paintsville.

The Green River Boys covered songs they had learned back home at funerals, church revivals, back porch guitar pulls, records, and live shows by Flatt and Scruggs in high school auditoriums. These were lyrics and music that still bore the refrains of Celtic ballads. Words that came from people who grubbed a life from mountains, hillsides, flats, and rills. "Oh, no I can't forget the hour/you're the only one mom/and sweeter than flowers," sang Reno and Smiley, World War II veterans, trying to make a living on the road singing bluegrass, Reno playing closer to the bridge on his banjo, taking the sound to sharper riffs and pull-offs. Bill Monroe casting in stone the high lonesome sounds. Ralph Stanley putting down the tones of the Clinch Mountains on records.

Mournful lyrics and tunes about mothers, death, and silver haired daddies sang and played by tattooed men unashamed to show tenderness and grief. *"Will There Be Sweethearts In Heaven,"* an old country ballad asks. These were the voices of the lonely and downtrodden, songs about people who had lived close to the core of life where they had seen hard rains beat down on the brown dirt that covered the graves of mothers, sisters, brothers, grandparents, and infants. Loved ones who took sick and died. Songs about rosewood caskets that took the cash from the year's tobacco crop to pay for.

The Green River Boys could sing these songs from the bleak earth because the lyrics and tunes came from the trials of their own lives. Long summer days in the fields working a cultivator behind sweating work horses. Edging through the redbrush to pick blackberries among copperhead and rattlesnake lairs. Salvaging a road-killed chicken for its edible parts. Skimming cream from a crock in the cellar for a Sunday dessert of strawberries. Tramping through cold winter snows and mud to milk a few scrawny cows. Watching their aging mother gather greens in a dishpan on an April day. Bumming rides into town on Saturdays, riding the running boards of rusted-out Fords and

Chevvies. Borrowing spoonfuls of whiskey from neighbors to treat sick parents with the flu. Taking small pleasures from the tender white violets that bloomed in May, a chew of homemade tobacco, or making over tiny babies at family reunions. They could bring an ephemeral truth to the songs of loneliness and death, because they were lonely and they had seen death up close. Simple phrases, "Mother's not dead she's, only sleeping," became epiphanies for men and women who sang and heard homemade bluegrass. These refrains were, as Maybelle Carter once said, "...older than nobody knows." The comfort they brought to those who sang them and those who heard them gave strength to carry people over and, finally, beyond sadness. They did for Appalachians the same thing black blues did for sharecroppers in Coahoma County, Mississippi.

Children of the hills still search these songs out. For they affirmed that there was love on earth and an even greater love for the saved in heaven where Jesus was. Whether it was at a burial, a prayer meeting, or in a beer joint, the same chords were struck and the same tonali-

Larry Varney collection

*Many folks from Kentucky, West Virginia, and southern Ohio, after moving north for work in the 1940s and 1950s, played weekend gigs in beer joints. Loretta Lynn, Dwight Yoakam, Ricky Scaggs, Bobby Bear, Jimmy Dickens, Mollie O'Day, Hawkshaw Hawkins, Larry Cordle, Keith Whitley, Melvin Goins, Patty Loveless, and others made it big. Shown: Larry Varney and friend from West Virginia at the Little Nashville Club, West Broad Street, Columbus, Ohio, circa 1955.*

ties came forth. The Green River Boys have long since broken up. Dave's Place was razed to make way for an interstate. Many of the families who took 23 North became Colum-

*Mary, Henry, and George Null at home near Waterloo, Ohio, circa 1910. Henry made music on an acoustic guitar as Mary and George listened. Home made entertainment was as common as cornbread.*

Duane Null collection

bus natives who now join their grandchildren for an MTV Unplugged performance. The bluegrass that went on to sweep college stages in the sixties has withdrawn to the summer festivals and the refurbished Rhyman. The lonesome sounds, however, won't die. Those of us who shared this music in our youth with families, friends, and neighbors still hear the high tenor harmonies in our heads and on CD players in our 4x4's. Alison Krauss steps forth in the 21st Century with vocal chords as fine as a Stradivarius. Sure, she's more likely to sing new tunes like, "You're the lucky one/I know that now" than stories of whiskey and blood running together. But somewhere in the set, even she will do a number or coax growls out of her fiddle that evoke memories of the smoke and beer of Dave's Place and the evolution of bluegrass.

# Moonshine Reflections

Beyond Fourteen Mile Mountain, whitewashed tree trunks and flower beds snuggled in worn tire casings set off the tiny houses perched on ledges along State Route 10. Dilapidated footbridges across the Guyandotte River swayed indolently in the dog-day heat. Newly washed clothes hung from lines strung between utility poles. Shoppers lounged in and out of the Fas-Chek market, and across the road Carver's Carry Out advertised Red Man and cold beer. The sky was pale blue and small, closed in by the mountains that embrace Harts Creek and its people.

The village of Harts, West Virginia, located in Lincoln County, seldom makes news beyond the encircling peaks. But in June of 1988, when the state police seized and destroyed a moonshine still, the Associated Press reported the incident across the country. Not that making moonshine—illegal, untaxed whiskey—was anything new in Lincoln County or, for that matter, anywhere in Appalachia. It was just that no raid had been heard of in a long time. Marijuana has become the region's largest cash crop and its most ominous illegal activity; controlling cannabis now absorbs the official energy once devoted to moonshine.

Down at the Dobie Shack, a crude lean-to building on Harts Creek Road, 65-year-old Dickie Dempsey was just back from an out-of-season squirrel hunt. He and four or five other men who had gathered for a game of five-card stud were subdued. They knew of several active stills up in the sticks; but they weren't talking, at least to strangers. It's been 20 years since Dempsey made whiskey. But he still remembers the time he got set up for a bust and wound up with three years' probation from a federal judge at Bluefield.

Brenda Koontz collection

*Moonshine still confiscated by authorities, West Virginia, circa 1930.*

Through the early years of the 19th century, hundreds of Scotch-Irish came into the southern Ohio plateau. From Jefferson County to Clermont along the Ohio past Washington, Lawrence, Scioto, and westward; from Holmes County through Hocking and Ross inland, southeastern Ohio, along with other parts of Appalachia—all became a bastion of Scotch-Irish folkways. Among these was the ancestral propensity to make, drink, and sell whiskey, and a disinclination, equally a part of their heritage, to pay taxes on it. Though not exclusively Scotch-Irish, this migration to the uplands was nearly so. In the places where the Scotch-Irish settled, the historical, cultural, and economic patterns that had made distilling a prominent domestic enterprise were abetted by geography, and they persisted.

The remote mountains and plateaus of Appalachia encompass 195,000 square miles, an area larger than England and Scotland combined. Stretching from New York State to northern Mississippi and from north-central Ohio to South Carolina, the Appalachians are the greatest mountain system in eastern North America. The Great Smoky, Blue Ridge, Cumberland, and Allegheny Mountains break upward among an endless array of creeks and rivers. North Carolina alone has 21 peaks that ascend higher than Mount Washington in New Hampshire.

The first settlers found a land of runs that flowed over limestone rocks and formed streams where the Cherokees fished for trout and catfish. Ginseng, mayapple, blackberries, and raspberries grew along the damp ravines. Locust, oak, black walnut, and other hardwood trees

*John and George Null gutting a hog in late fall, Webster Road, Gallia County, Ohio, near Waterloo.*

Duane Null collection

studded the slopes; killdeers and ruffed grouse gamboled through the dense foliage. But rich bottom land was scarce, travel was arduous, and communication was difficult. No one knows why these Scotch-Irish drifters didn't move on to the lush flat lands of the Midwest. It is certain they had little knowledge of what lay beyond the hills and valleys. Their history had equipped them with survival skills that would wrest some bounty even from this rugged land.

On the periphery of this Appalachian homeland, Scottown, Ohio, is separated from Harts, West Virginia, by ninety miles of crooked, two-lane blacktop. Near Scottown, up creeks with names like Buckeye, Sandfork, Turkey, and Federal, smoke from working stills lifted into the night. Along ridges called Greasy, Tick, Wilson, and Tagg, fermenting cornmeal bubbled in mash boxes, and 100-proof white lightning dripped from worm cocks. Tagg Hollow got its name from a man whose character and physique were as rugged as the great trees that grew tall along the flats, a fair enough system for an unmapped country. When the county surveyors, road builders, village stores, and township trustees came, place-names like Buckeye Hollow, Polkadotte, and Greasy Ridge were already there. And so were the families who planted corn in grubbed-out flats, foraged their livestock in the woods, cured a little tobacco, made whiskey, and trapped muskrats along Indian Guyan Creek. They made their own coffins and staked out family cemeteries on ridge-top knolls. As with the child in Wordsworth's poem, "We Are Seven," even the dead were still members of the family.

From Shadyside in Belmont County, Ohio, to Matewan in Mingo County, West Virginia, to bloody Hazard in Perry County, Kentucky— set apart by dialect, custom, and physical isolation—they came to be what Edgar Allen Poe described in 1845 as a "fierce and uncouth race of men." The observation was true enough, as far as it went. Clannish, suspicious of the unfamiliar, quick to resent a slight, they were at the same time generous, forthright, and unswerving in their loyalties.

Tina Bryan collection

*Family working in corn field, Ohio River Valley, circa 1940.*

Most of what they had, they made themselves. Every man might be called on to be his own blacksmith, gunsmith, carpenter, cobbler, miller, or dentist. They farmed on forty-degree slopes. The women worked in the fields, raised vegetable gardens, fed chickens, cut firewood, tended the children, nursed the sick, cooked, made quilts, milked cows, and, if they were able, read the Bible. The young children played in rock houses and made grapevine swings; the older ones worked beside their parents. They were poor and ignorant of the world beyond their hills; but a simple dignity made them impervious to ridicule of their ways, and their word was a bond of truth.

Throughout Appalachia, whiskey making as a family enterprise expanded in the early part of the nineteenth century. The liquor was a perfect, natural product—pure corn and branch water, cooked in copper, and fired with wood. The church was ambivalent. With many people depending on whiskey for cash or barter income, preachers were understandably reluctant to criticize the distillers. Indeed, the cleric might take his salary in whiskey, or even, if one of the stock figures of 19th-century genre fiction had a real-life prototype, supplement his income by his own weekday labors at the still.

Whiskey making persisted for practical as well as cultural reasons. The process converted a relatively low-value grain crop into an easily marketable commodity. Whiskey was easy to store and move. It was used for medicinal purposes: camphor diluted with moonshine served in place of smelling salts. Held on a rotten tooth, it was a pain-killer. Babies with the croup were held over fumes of moonshine burned with turpentine to relieve lung congestion. Mixed with rock candy and glycerine, it was taken for bronchitis. Moonshine girded the hunter against the chill of the winter woods and the roustabout against the river damp of the steamboat landing. For the traveler it was proof against the precarious hospitalities of an unfamiliar road.

In the post-Civil War years, a growing temperance movement, tax enforcement, and economies of scale accelerated a domination of the distilling industry by a relatively few large concerns. The mountain operator was little affected by these trends, except that he carried his equipment and supplies on his back or a horse-drawn sled, through the redbrush and cockleburs, to a spot hidden from traffic along the trails.

The efforts of men and women who opposed drinking for religious and moral reasons were relentless. In Highland County, Ohio, Eliza Jane Thompson started the Women's Temperance Crusade in 1873. Her campaign closed all the liquor outlets in Hillsboro and led to the founding of the Women's Christian Temperance Union. Another Ohio organization, the Anti-Saloon League, soon gained national prominence. The Prohibition party, the National Temperance Society, the Methodist and Presbyterian churches, Carrie Nation, and, later, evangelist Billy Sunday railed against drinking. County after county, and state after state, voted themselves dry.

Will Rogers's prediction that Oklahoma would stay dry as long as enough people could stagger to the polls to keep it that way came true for the entire nation. Prohibition was a bonanza for the illegal distillers, causing the value of moonshine to rise from three to twenty-two dollars per gallon. Many a moonshining mountaineer expanded

Gallia County Historical Society

*Waterloo Methodist Campground, circa 1890, a place where "drys" congregated.*

his operations and entered more distant markets. Increased demand motivated some whiskey makers to adulterate the product and stimulated production by newcomers to the craft who were both unskilled and unscrupulous.

Ohio's most prolific moonshiners operated at the southern tip of the state in Lawrence County. Crooked in a bend of the Ohio River, its several ports furnished sin of several varieties to a raffish motley of steamboaters and river travelers. It was just a 15-minute ferry ride away from railroad towns that were beginning to develop in Kentucky and West Virginia; yet, except for Ironton, it was remote from internal population centers where any reformist impulse might gain momentum. Lawrence County early on developed a reputation for bawdiness that persisted into the twentieth century. Patrons who called on Tom Lewis at his Scottown grocery store could buy a bottle of Dr. Le Gear's Flatulent Colic Medicine or slide nickels into a genuine slot machine. Even during World War II and into the 1950s, slot machines and other gambling activities were wide open from Johnny Faulkner's barbershop in Miller to the gaudy Continental Club in Chesapeake, where uniformed deputy sheriffs moonlighted as armed guards.

Across Appalachia, Prohibition, hard times, and the automobile helped make numerous back country roadhouses a Saturday night institution. Black jazz musicians drifted up the two-lane gravel roads from Coahoma County, Mississippi, through east Tennessee into Kentucky, West Virginia, and southern Ohio. Duke Ellington, Count Basie, Bessie Smith, Tiny Bradshaw, and others perfected their smooth and smoky riffs at weekend gigs in windowless, cinder-block buildings where white patrons mixed with black. West Virginia jazz musician Nat Reese described the scene: "Well, someone was killed down there every week. There was gambling, hustling, numbers playing, prostitution. You could buy whiskey, any kind you wanted: Scotch, bourbon, good moonshine, bad moonshine." Through the years, road houses with their live bands, dance floors sprinkled with rosin, and gravel parking lots provided a lively mixture of fun and trouble for Kentuckians, West Virginians, and southern Ohioans. Long gone from Route 7 in Lawrence County, Ohio, the Blue Moon, the Rome Beauty Inn, and the Hi-De-Ho remain in the dusty memories of the 1950s. Between sets played by local hillbilly pickers, patrons went outside to their cars to sip from jars of moonshine.

W. Allen Cross, a former usher at the Keith-Albee Theater in Huntington, West Virginia, told about the times when bootleg moonshine was run in from Scottown and from adjacent areas in West Virginia and Kentucky. It was sold in a bootlegging room over the State Theater and at a variety of beer joints on the Second Avenue strip where the whorehouses were located. It was available in bottles and also by the drink for 25 cents a two-ounce shot. The bootleggers had routes and divided the territory up in order to avoid internal conflict. When a seller brought in bad whiskey, however, one of his colleagues would usually tip off the revenue agents. According to Cross, most local lawmen took rake-offs, but the federal men were harder to deal with. He noted that many of his customers preferred moonshine to what they called store-bought, or red whiskey, and that many drinkers just wanted to go on a jag once in a while over a weekend. Men and their dates would come in and buy a horse quart, get rooms in a cheap hotel, and party all night. Cross used to sell whiskey to a chemistry professor at Marshall College named Joe Pollard, an MIT graduate who liked what he called "slick whiskey." Pollard, skeptical about the proof of the whiskey Cross sold him, ran a chemical analysis on it and found it to be 105. He was, thereafter, a regular customer.

Cross said that "...the people up in the mountains thought it was not illegal because for generations they'd been making their own whiskey like they'd been making their own clothes. Hell, it was just a form of life. No one cared." Another former bootlegger said that many professional people requested that they be notified when the good stuff came in. He also told of a visit to a relative in Logan County, West Virginia. After church services and dinner, his uncle took him over to a barrel of whiskey and offered him a drink. When asked if he was afraid of the law, the uncle said, "Up in this holler, we make our own laws."

On Greasy Ridge, in Lawrence County, a farmer and part-time moonshiner named Glen Harland had a similar ethic. As the winter winds whipped down through Buckeye Hollow, it was a common sight to see Harland bouncing along Greasy Ridge Road in a Model T Ford, his sharp features partially hidden under a gray felt hat. He had a rural whiskey route with regular stops. Neatly dressed and friendly, his whiskey packed in a suitcase, he resembled a Raleigh man more than a moonshiner. An officer stopped Harland once and asked what he had in the suitcase. "Hell, it's full of moonshine, what do you think it is?" Harland quipped. The officer just winked and passed the comment off as a joke. Harland used to tell his neighbors that half the pleasure in selling whiskey was being able to flimflam the local constables. The give-and-take between lawman and lawbreaker was sometimes turned by mutual respect into an almost amicable rivalry. Former revenue agent Bob Downey said he and his cohorts used to drive by the homes of moonshiners on Sunday afternoons, sit, talk, and swap cigarettes with them, then go out and chase them the next night. Many of them, he said, were "pillars of their communities and so supportive of one another that when seized cars were offered for sale at sheriff's auctions, no one would make a bid." There were times, however, when skirmishes brought mayhem.

"Joe Rigney had bad luck today," Olaf Murray told a moonshiner named Bill Hayes one hot July night in 1952. He had. Constable Rigney, described by Hayes as a person with "more nerve than brains," had been dead several hours when Murray stopped to buy a fifth of whiskey. A few days earlier, Rigney had confronted Murray, a world champion horse puller, and two companions at the Lawrence County Fair. With the blur of lights from the Tilt-a-Whirl as a backdrop, Rigney accused Murray of possessing moonshine. An angry exchange followed, and Murray and his party returned to their homes near Mercerville in Gallia County. The next day an embarrassed Rigney obtained a warrant for Murray's arrest and attempted to serve it. When he walked into Murray's yard, a shotgun blast fatally wounded him. Gallia Sheriff George Ehman's deputies refused to go after Murray, but he finally surrendered and served five years in the Ohio Penitentiary. Incidents of high drama such as this were rare occurrences in the plateau. But in some mountain counties of Kentucky and Tennessee, four or five moonshine-related homicides per month were reported during the Prohibition years. In Leslie County, Kentucky, three sheriffs were run out of Hyden, the county seat, in a single week by gangs of armed moonshiners. The violence in those regions for years attracted on-the-scene reporters from major newspapers, including the *New York Times*. Federal agents continued to press on with their task throughout Appalachia, including the Ohio plateau, and dozens of them were killed in the line of duty during the moonshine wars of the 1920s.

Bill Hayes made and sold whiskey in the Scottown area for more than 30 years. In the late 1930s, in an attempt to get out of the whiskey business, he went to Ironton and applied for a job with the Works

Progress Administration, created by the Roosevelt administration. When the interviewer asked how he was earning his living, Hayes told him he was bootlegging. "Well, go on back and do that, you don't need a job," he was told. Such was Lawrence County during the Depression, where Bill Holschuh, a local storekeeper, would grin and ask Hayes if it were a good year for blackberry jelly when he bought five 100-pound sacks of sugar in a single purchase. Hayes described whiskey making as hard work: bags of sugar, corn, barrels, tools, and the still, which weighed 50 pounds or more, had to be carried by hand or pulled by horses back into the woods. A supply of water was necessary, and several hours of labor were required to prepare the mash. The distillation process took five hours of intense work by at least one man. And all this work had to be done under possible surveillance by the law. Many times mash and other supplies left overnight were destroyed by someone in the neighborhood. Other times the whiskey didn't turn out right and was worthless. And then there was federal court in Cincinnati where Hayes had to appear after a government

Dale Holschuh collection

*Scottown, Ohio, seen here in the 1950 flood, was a center for moonshine and bootlegging until 1960. When Bill Hayes went to Ironton, Ohio, in 1940 to sign up for work on the WPA (Works Progress Administration), he told the clerk he made whiskey. He was told to go on back home and continue to do that; he didn't need a job.*

Author's collection

*Rock cellar, Williams Creek, Gallia County, Ohio. These were common through the 19th century. Hewed out of solid rock, cellars held crocks of fresh milk and cream, apples, potatoes, jars of home-canned goods, maybe a horse quart of moonshine. Two miles from Crown City, inland culture had its own amenities.*

man saw him make a two-gallon sale. He had been charged twice before, and his lawyer on this occasion expressed reservations about keeping him out of jail. Hayes had already paid the lawyer $200. He asked his lawyer if he thought another $500 that he had on him would do any good. The lawyer told him he could make a strong effort for that, and with a guilty plea, Hayes handed over $300.

Both Hayes and Dickie Dempsey, on occasion, made large sales of 50 or more gallons of moonshine to a single customer. Dempsey told of having to dig around his barn and fields for hours in order to fill one order for an Ohio bootlegger. But the last act of the classic moonshine drama was slowly ebbing to a close. Even though Ohio gave up 61 stills to federal revenue agents as late as 1969, moonshine production has been on a steady decline. Only three stills were seized by federal agents in 1987. But it is still made in numerous hills and hollows in the region.

Harts Creek natives who have moved away still pick up a few gallons of moonshine on weekend visits, running it down the hillbilly highway to Charlotte or Winston-Salem. They'll sell a half-gallon for $16, drink the rest, and feel homesick for Lincoln County. Claude Preecer stays behind, keeps his pickup truck serviced, and waits for the mountain laurel to bloom again.

On a warm September Sunday in 1988, Dickie Dempsey fired up a cigarette and relaxed in the Dobie Shack on Harts Creek Road. His smile was subtle and sly and came easily as he talked. Dempsey has lived on Harts Creek all his life except for a brief hiatus in Detroit, which he hated. His father was a renowned local moonshiner; his paternal grandfather was a Baptist preacher who spent his lifetime trying to rid Harts Creek of whiskey and other traditional sins of the flesh. One of his uncles, convicted for moonshining, served two years in the West Virginia State Prison at Moundsville.

Dickie Dempsey started making whiskey when he was 25 and continued until 1965 when, at 40, he tired of the work and quit. During the 15 years he made and sold whiskey, he was busted once. In 1964 a federal agent posing as a coal mine boss from Logan County set him up. He was arrested and later pleaded guilty in federal court in Bluefield and was placed on probation for three years. Afterward, he continued to bootleg for a few years. Dempsey made whiskey for a living; it was, he said, "better than grubbing out new ground to try to farm anything." The Harts Creek valley was not a friendly place for farmers. Small bottoms that flood, steep mountains more suitable for gathering ginseng. Moonshine sold for ten dollars per gallon in the 1950s, a net profit for Dempsey of four dollars. Most of the mountain people preferred it to what they call red whiskey. He sold moonshine to local law officers, to the high sheriff, and to judges who sat on the bench in Logan and Mingo counties.

Dempsey's neighbors and relatives portrayed him as a good father, an unselfish person who provided for his family the best he could through some very hard times. He discouraged his sons from making moonshine, and they have chosen to follow that advice. Although he still drinks 10 to 12 beers a day, his religious beliefs are fundamental. When asked about the morality of drinking, his response was, "One swallow is the same as half-a-gallon. You can't drink and be a Christian." Bill Hayes became a born-again Christian and a successful truck farmer until his death in 1998. He was one of the hardest working men in the Scottown area. Even in his eighties and nineties, he worked several farms from spring onions to fall turnips. It was said on the Huntington Produce market that Hayes was the first to arrive and the last to leave during the growing and selling season. In his long years he never came to trust the federal government.

The small amount of moonshine now available on Harts Creek and in Scottown is made by younger men. Parts of Appalachia remain isolated, and many of the people are still poor. But those who have chosen to stay in Lincoln County are more likely to be found among the Friday night basketball crowd at Harts High School than up some hollow making moonshine. And if there is anything to drink behind the seats of their Ford Broncos, it is probably a six-pack of cold beer or a fifth of Jim Beam. If there's illegal peddling, it's probably weed.

# The Story of Bevo Francis

Downtown Raleigh, North Carolina, was aglow with the red and green blinking lights of Christmastime. On Fayetteville Street, shoppers strolled past Neiman's Jewelers and the Roscoe-Griffin shoe store. A mild breeze drifted across the Piedmont. Cloudy skies kept the temperature at 60. Moviegoers left the Ambassador Theater, whites emerging under the marquee and blacks from the "colored entrance" three doors up the street, after a screening of *Thunder Over The Plains* starring Randolph Scott. Gene Autry's *Rudolph The Red-Nosed Reindeer* rattled from tinny speakers above the Salvation Army booth on the main thoroughfare. And over on Morgan Street, in the Term Billiard Parlor, pool sharps danced among the mahogany tables.

Across town on Cates Avenue, inside the Reynolds Coliseum, the scoreboard billed the contestants for the 7:30 p.m. basketball game: Rio Grande and Wake Forest. The date was December 24, 1953, the closing night of a two-day holiday series with North Carolina State and Wake Forest pairing off against Rio Grande College and the Peoria Caterpillars, national amateur Athletic Union champions. In the first night's play, the Rio Grande Redmen had lost to the NC State Wolfpack, 77 to 92. Now the Ohioans were scheduled against Wake's Deacons, the defending Atlantic Coast Conference champions.

Although he had coached his team to a 39 - 0 season the year before, John Newton "Newt" Oliver's boast that Rio Grande could move up from competition like the Cincinnati Bible Seminary to play major basketball powerhouses still needed shoring up. They recently had defeated Providence College and the University of Miami, and they came within a point at Villanova. But in a much-ballyhooed game at

Madison Square Garden, they lost to Adelphi by seven points. And back home on the college campus, administrators were vexed. Oliver's aggressive, hustling style and the fame of his star player, six-foot-nine-inch Clarence "Bevo" Francis, had created a public image at odds with the school's traditional role as an academic and spiritual haven for future teachers and preachers.

A boisterous crowd awaited the Redmen in the brick-and-steel coliseum. Their red and white satin uniforms gleamed under the lights as they took to the hardwood amidst a standing ovation from spectators hungry for a look at Francis, the legendary shooter who had scored 116 points in a single game. During the listless first half, neither Francis nor Wake star Dick Hemric could find the range. Francis and Wayne Wiseman, a guard from Waterloo, Ohio, carried Rio Grande to a 41 - 40 lead late in the third quarter. The rest of the game was classic basketball. The score was tied 10 times, but, with less than two minutes left, the Deacons led 65 - 61. The scrappy Redmen came back. Wiseman scored a field goal, and guard Bill Ripperger stole the ball and dropped in a basket to tie the score. At the five-second mark, Wiseman worked the ball to Bevo, who turned, jumped, and scored as the whistle blew. The Redmen were mobbed at center court. Rio Grande had defeated Wake Forest, 67 - 65, and Bevo had outscored Hemric 32 to 24. Even the irreverent Oliver, arm around Bevo's waist as they left the arena, had a feeling that Providence was on his side. Amidst laughter and joking on the bumpy plane ride back to Charleston, West Virginia, the last thought in anyone's mind was that the controversy swirling around Oliver and Francis would break up the team and leave a long string of unhealed wounds.

For Newt Oliver, a scrawny kid growing up on Spruce Avenue in Byesville, Ohio, basketball was a way to forever leave the coal fields. As a Rio Grande player, he led the nation in scoring in 1947. After college he coached for two years under superintendent Charles E. Davis at Upper Sandusky High School. Oliver produced winning teams, but his scraps with other coaches and a reluctance to fawn over community leaders created ill will. On a sour note, he moved on to the Ohio River town of Wellsville, where, on a sticky August day in 1951, on the high school football field, he first set his eyes on Bevo Francis. It was characteristic of Oliver that where others saw another good schoolboy athlete, he saw a man with the potential to become one of the most famous players in basketball history.

Bevo Francis grew up on a small farm in Hammondsville, Ohio. The seventh child in a family that was often on relief, he was immersed early on in a working-class, rural culture that included hoeing corn, slopping hogs, shoveling manure, and picking blackberries. Fun time during these depression years meant grapevine swings, following hounds in search of rabbits, raccoons, and listening to Henry Aldrich on the radio. But when the 12-year-old Bevo discovered basketball, everything else took second place. He and the boys he roughhoused with talked a local farmer, Pete Cope, into turning his barn into a lighted basketball court. The barn became a second home to Bevo and the others he coaxed to play with him. On weekends, the boys brought food, drink, and blankets, and, after playing into the night, slept in the hayloft.

When Bevo was 16, his family moved to a modest house on Main Street in Wellsville. His transfer from Irondale High School, however, resulted in a charge from the Ohio High School Athletic Association that he had been illegally recruited. Declared ineligible for high school ball, he played with a variety of independent clubs. He spent long, arduous hours perfecting his smooth and graceful moves with a basketball, unperturbed by the authorities's decision to extend his ineligibility for another year. He was a 19-year-old junior, with a single year of eligibility left, when he finally took to the gymnasium with Newt Oliver.

The 1951-52 season at Wellsville High School brought Bevo his first widespread acclaim. In a 19-game campaign, he scored 612 points, averaging 30.6 per game. In six of the Tigers' 20 games, he outscored the entire opposing team. He was recognized by the International

News Service and the Associated Press for his basketball prowess. He was the first Ohio high school athlete to receive the Helms Foundation award, and 63 colleges and universities tried to recruit him. He chose Rio Grande when Oliver's old boss, Charles Davis, who was then president of Rio Grande College, invited them both down for the 1952 - 53 season. And the people around Wellsville wondered why they wanted to go as far away as Texas when Ohio had so many good schools. It might as well have been Texas for Bevo as he, wife and baby by his side, traveled southward down the crooked State Route 7 that follows the Ohio River—off to college at age 20, a credit-and-a-half short of a high school diploma.

One-hundred-thirty years before Bevo turned the sharp curve on State Route 35 in Gallia County that passes Rio Grande, Nehemiah Atwood and his wife, Permilia, built a brick house and tavern on the Pleasant Valley Road, a stagecoach route from Gallipolis to Chillicothe. They became wealthy from farm products and the tavern. In the winter of 1850, Reverend Ira E. Haning, a 25-year-old minister of the Freewill Baptist faith, rode into town from Athens. Haning's hellfire and brimstone sermons were so successful that more than 200 area residents gave their souls to the Lord, the Atwoods being among the saved. Mr. Atwood became so enthralled with Haning's message that he gave money for Haning to build the Calvary Baptist Church in Rio Grande and even became a deacon. The friendship between Atwood and Haning continued until 1869 when Atwood, age 77, died.

Haning had urged the Atwoods to provide money for a college, and, after Nehemiah's death, Permilia remarried the next year and preserved the thought of financing a school where young men could be trained to preach. For the next five years, she and her husband developed plans for the college, and in 1874 the cornerstone was laid for the first building. Two years later Permilia died, leaving her entire estate to the college. Haning's call to sanctified education brought forth the 15 students and four professors who occupied Atwood and Boarding Halls in the fall of 1876. In that placid setting, students from the region were invited to approach God and nature with devout piety.

Down through the years, Rio Grande continued as a refuge apart from a world of sin and materialism. The Baptist church maintained its support, and presidents were either active preachers or, at least, dedicated to the Christian principles of frugality, capitalism, modesty, and chastity. The College Christian Association, formed in 1881, was the most influential student organization on campus. Chapel was required weekly, and glee clubs, intramural athletics, operettas, and the Welsh *Eisteddfod* festivals emerged as diversions from the rigors of study and prayer. Poets, visionaries, aesthetes, dandies, and bohemians were advised to study elsewhere.

The village of Rio Grande and the college evolved as one. Students and faculty brought money to town that helped support the merchants and rooming houses. Quaint vernacular houses surrounded the central campus. Many residents rented rooms to students, and the Allen House served three meals a day to its boarders. Raccoon Township and the village were dry, and those few who enjoyed a glass of wine with meals or sipped hot toddies on winter nights were discreet. Young people played dare base, went for sleigh rides in the snow, swam at Cora Park in summer, played rook, and square danced at the Masonic Hall in Centerville. The village, almost seeming to deny the inevitability of death while proclaiming a glory land afterward, didn't even support an undertaker. Doors were left unlocked. No one can recall a murder or any infamous event in the village's history. The most memorable incident happened when Atwood Hall, an imposing structure with a four-sided clock tower, burned to the ground in 1917. By 1950 Rio Grande had grown to a population of 350, most of whom voted Republican.

Sports activities at Rio Grande had a low profile. Competitive football was introduced in 1915, and men's basketball followed a year later. Scheduling was informal, and at times high school players filled out the roster. The 1920 team photograph shows just six players dressed. By 1941 Rio Grande was playing a full schedule of small schools and independent teams. During World War II, when enrollment dropped as low as 44, basketball barely survived. After the war, a series of coaches struggled to keep the sport alive.

By 1951 Rio Grande was in debt, losing enrollment, and on the verge of being cast out by the American Baptist Association. Rio Grande alumnus, Don Allen, who had parlayed a job selling used cars in Gallipolis into a string of Chevrolet dealerships from New York to Florida, urged the trustees to offer the presidency to Charles Davis. Gray-suited, with cuffed trousers that broke hard over brown wing-tips, Davis was an imposing figure. In his youth he played professional football with the Ironton Tanks, bringing down Jim Thorpe in a memorable game. He was a ground officer with the Army Air Corps in World War II and had achieved some notoriety for initiating all-night, supervised high school proms. The many-sided Davis led cheers at pep rallies, prayed in chapel, and shared smokes and wine with friends and alumni during social functions. Rio Grande's first modern president, his vision was primarily secular and pragmatic. So, in the summer of 1952, when he offered Newt Oliver an employment package containing $3,500 the first year, five weeks off in the summer, and the title of Director of Physical Education, in return for Bevo Francis and coaching services, it was hailed as a monumental event. Oliver talked Don Allen out of some scholarship money and began recruiting players.

Newt Oliver welcomed the September heat and the lonesome hum of the cicadas in the oak trees that lined the walkways around Community Hall. The new Redmen basketball team was complete and in practice daily. Three returning players and seven recruits from regional high schools supported Bevo. Oliver, whose speech and motions were sharp and intense, had no trouble intimidating young men more accustomed to the twangy, laid back, local drawl. And a new message was forthcoming: in addition to playing for camaraderie and fellowship, their goals included an undefeated season, a 100-point-per-game average, getting the ball to Bevo each time he was open, and bookings in large arenas.

Newt Oliver collection

*Clarence Bevo Francis at Rio Grande College, 1952.*

Bevo Francis enrolled in the local high school and matriculated as a full-time college student majoring in secondary education. Oliver received Ohio College Association's approval for Bevo's eligibility and joined the NCAA Service Bureau to have game statistics legitimized. Eighteen games were inherited from commitments made the year before. As winter rolled around, Oliver worked the telephone in search of publicity and more games. Over in New Dorm, with Oliver beyond earshot, team members griped about the rigorous drills and wondered who could be crazy enough to think Rio Grande would ever play in Madison Square Garden. And in the late night hours, ignoring the coach's warnings, Wayne Wiseman and Jim McKenzie played quarter limit draw poker and pulled on Pall Malls.

Ninety fans filed into Community Hall—players called it the Hog Pen—on the crisp autumn evening of November 8. This traditional first game against an alumni team resulted in a lopsided win; Bevo scored 44. Over the next few weeks, Rio Grande played five home games. Oliver raised ticket prices from 50 to 75 cents, and, when loyal supporters complained, he told them to prepare for even higher prices. Oliver's scramble for media attention paid off when Waynesburg College of Pennsylvania came to campus. Dave Diles, a former local reporter working for the Associated Press in Columbus, was in the press box. The Redmen clowned through the game in farmer's overalls after being taunted as hayseeds by Waynesburg and won 108 to 70. Bevo had 46. Against Wilberforce College, Bevo scored 69, just two points less than the opposition. Playing eight of their next 10 games on the road, with barely enough money to buy gas for their two antiquated station wagons, they continued to win. By the end of December, when they defeated Cumberland College of Kentucky, Rio Grande had scored 1,558 points while their opponents had 1,101. Bevo had 743 himself, an average of 46.5 per game. President Davis, in one of Diles's reports that finally caught the attention of the national press, called Bevo "a big asset both to the team and the school." And while the January cold gripped the campus, deserted by the team and other students for holiday break, even Oliver's skeptics began to take notice.

The lonesome, honky-tonk beat of a Hank Williams song playing on the jukebox and the clank of the pinball machine in Frank Denny's restaurant signaled the students' return to campus. The second semester broke fast for the Redmen. They played their first game of 1953 at Findlay College. The win was close, but a good team effort and Bevo's 44 points before a crowd of 1,500 was played up in the local paper. Two days later, back at Community Hall, Ashland Junior College of Kentucky was the opponent in a packed house of 150. This small crowd witnessed an event that made sports history and switched on the floodlights of celebrity for Oliver and Francis. Bevo scored 116 points, making 47 field goals and 22 free throws. Fifty-five of his points came in the final quarter.

Wire services, television, radio, and the Army's *Stars and Stripes* sent accounts of the feat around the world. Within three weeks *Time, Saga,* and *Life* magazine, *Movietone News,* the *Dave Garroway* television show, the *Sporting News,* and major daily newspapers across the country did features on Bevo and Rio Grande College. When Bevo was asked for a comment, he said, "I always seem to have one hot night a year." Not since George Mikan of DePaul in the 1940s had a player attracted the kind of attention Bevo Francis began to receive. Within a fortnight, the little village where squirrels romped undisturbed was thronged with national photographers, reporters, and film crews. An ecstatic Oliver egged the journalists on and argued that Bevo was better than Kentucky's Bill Spivey and that they would play any team in the country. When Oliver was asked about his coaching style, he gave an answer both candid and cynical: "I have four or five systems but I usually use one where Bevo gets every shot."

Oliver seized the day, seeking higher stakes as offers came from large arenas. A game with Bliss College was moved to the Aquinas High School gym in Columbus where 2,500 people squeezed in, and many were turned away. A television crew from the *Today* show documented the contest as Bevo surpassed Johnny O'Brian's NAIA season record of 1,051. Oliver rescheduled games to large arenas in Troy, Cleveland, and Columbus. Take-home money approached $5,000 per game. Oakland City College of Indiana, however, was unhappy when Oliver broke a deal with them and took the Redmen to the Cleveland Arena for $2,500 and a percentage of the gate. The Oakland athletic director complained and, without consulting Oliver, Davis sent them a $500 check to cover a $75 contract.

When the Redmen played George Steinbrenner's Lockbourne Air Force Base team, ticket scalpers sold $1 tickets for $5. When they took on Cedarville College in Troy's Hobart Arena, 66 newspapers, *Life* magazine, and *Paramount* newsreels covered the game. Cedarville coach Floyd Reese tried a stall. During the first half, in front of a booing crowd, the Redmen put on warm-up suits, matched pennies thrown on the floor, and gave radio interviews. Reese continued to stall until half-time, when Cedarville's athletic director, fearing a riot, ordered the team to play. Bevo's 38 points, in the 66 - 29 win, outscored the entire Cedarville club. Two weeks later, Oliver took his team back to Wellsville to play Pikeville College in the high school gym. The game highlighted a weekend of celebrations for the town's most famous citizen, and after scoring 1,341 points in college competition, he was awarded a diploma from Wellsville High School. Back in Rio Grande, the administrators caucused.

Charlie Davis, as he liked to be called, had come to Rio Grande from a long career in the public schools. As a school superintendent, he was good at backslapping and ingratiating himself with board members and community leaders on the chicken dinner circuit, church functions, and meetings at the Rotary Clubs. But he was now caught in a tough situation between some faculty members, former president Dean W. A. Lewis, and Oliver. Lewis was a Christian traditionalist and a village hero who several times had rescued the college from oblivion. He was not about to stand by while Newt Oliver damaged the school's good name and what he thought was a sideshow put on by sports freaks. The handsome, mustachioed Davis hated discord and did his best to soft-pedal the controversy. This was a style that had served him well. Listening, mediating, compromising, seeking political solutions. Hearty handshakes, charisma, middle-of-the-road. But now he was dealing with issues larger than prom nights, bond issues, and the length of skirts on high school girls. With Oliver pushing out into unknown territory, and Dean Lewis trying to maintain the mossback conservatism of a bygone era, would Davis's flexible personality be enough? Near the end of January, Davis, who was usually ignored by reporters sniffing out stories about Bevo and Oliver, began to back away from the coach. Alluding to the traumatic point-shaving scandal of 1951, when players from New York City area schools as well as Bradley, Kentucky, and Toledo were implicated in deals with gamblers, Davis said, "We've seen too much of the evils of big-time basketball. We're just as proud of our gospel teams and deputation groups as we are of Bevo and the basketball team." He admitted, however, that the basketball income was helping the financially strapped college, and he welcomed the prospect of a bid from the National Invitational Tournament committee. Supporting Davis, Dean Lewis commented on the team's schedule, "It keeps them away from campus a lot. They're not as sharp as they should be."

But the media's focus remained on Bevo. Sportswriters called him "the most amazing thing to hit sports pages in years," "the most outstanding basketball player in the world today," and "the scarecrow kid with the amazing shooting eye." Milton Gross of the *New York Post,* who saw the Lockbourne game, was more reserved, calling Rio Grande's opposition "shadowy." Bevo, he wrote, "...has one good shot—a jump-push from 15 to 20 feet. He has no feints, no left hand ability, and makes few tap-ins." He concluded, however, that Bevo "...could fill in with any varsity team I've seen this year." When a reporter asked Oliver if his strategy of having teammates feed Bevo was making a farce of the records, he said, "No. High scoring is what the fans like. What about home runs in baseball? You going to limit those?" Bevo, still the humble country boy, remained nonplused by the attention.

By mid-February, speculation began to center on whether Rio Grande would be invited to play in the NIT in Madison Square Garden. Asa Bushnell, chairman of the tournament, knew that Rio Grande would be a good box-office attraction, and there was clamor from the media to bring them to New York City. But the fact that Rio Grande had built its reputation against small-school competition left Bushnell in a vexing situation. When he told the press that teams using freshmen would be considered, he was obviously leaving the door open for Bevo, but he made no commitment. The ever optimistic Oliver backed out of a charity date because the game conflicted with the Garden tournament and announced that Ned Irish, NIT promoter, wanted Rio Grande.

The Redmen continued their frantic pace on the road with seven easy wins before returning to Community Hall for the season's last home game, against Bluefield, West Virginia. Although Oliver angered local supporters by again raising ticket prices, 400 people crowded into the gym. Again, Davis expressed chagrin over the national hoopla and told Oliver that faculty members felt the team was missing too many classes. Oliver's response was terse: Davis should be pleased that magazines such as *Life* and *Time* were covering the school for the first time in history, and that they could pray there all day every Sunday, and they would still be head over heels in debt on Monday morning. When Davis said he didn't want the tail to wag the dog, Oliver replied, "Hell, there ain't no dog here." Davis's jealousy of Oliver and Bevo and their good fortune, as seen by a contemporary insider, seemed evident. But still when the team got new warm-up jackets, he demanded one for himself.

Moving toward the 39th and final game of the season and still hoping for post-season play, Oliver and Bevo were invited to a luncheon in New York City by the Metropolitan Association of Basketball Writers. After a press conference, they appeared on local radio and television, watched an NBA game at the Armory, and posed for pictures with Nat "Sweetwater" Clifton. Bevo appeared on the *Ed Sullivan* show. The exhilaration of the trip was dampened, however, when they received word that Seton Hall had received the coveted NIT bid. From

New York they flew to Cleveland for the season finale against Wilberforce. The crowd of 10,000 gathered for a Cleveland Arena doubleheader featuring Seton Hall gave Bevo a standing ovation for his 54 points in a game the Redmen won, 109 - 55. Seton Hall coach Honey Russell told a reporter "Bevo could make any team in the country today. That Rio Grande has a fine team."

Rio Grande received invitations to play in the NAIA tournament and East-West College All-Star Classic, but President Davis, following the policy enacted earlier by the school's athletic council, turned them down. Bevo was allowed to appear in a half-time shooting exhibition. The statistics for the Redmen for the 1952 - 53 season included a record of 39 and 0, the best in one season for any college. They averaged 101 points per game, played before 80,000 people, and placed 26th on the Associated Press national collegiate basketball team poll. Bevo's statistics included 1,954 points, 538 free throws, a 116-point game, first team selection by the Helms Athletic Foundation, and second team United Press All-American. At the spring basketball banquet in Gallipolis, Coach Frank Leahy of Notre Dame spoke and presented the team with the U.S. Rubber Company award as the most improved college team in the nation. Although the banquet pleasantries seemed to signify a truce between Oliver and Davis, Bevo was forced by Professor Clara Poston to leave early and drive to Dayton where he was assigned to speak to a Sunday school class the next morning. The final blow was delivered by the National Association of Basketball Coaches, led by Frank Cappon of Princeton University. At their convention in Kansas City, the NABC, with full support from Ohio State's Floyd Stahl, expressed alarm at the level of competition being used to compile athletic records. The new standards, which were accepted by the NCAA, recommended that official records include only games played against four-year, accredited colleges. Although Stahl warned against reflecting on Bevo Francis's credibility and called him a "...common people's All-American," he supported the committee in making the resolution retroactive. The Redmen's records were thus reduced to 12 - 0, and Bevo's record dropped to 580 points, a per-game average of 48.3. This decision was the most publicized of its kind since Jim Thorpe was deprived of Olympic medals in 1911. Oliver withdrew his team from the NCAA and joined the NAIA which accepted the records. When a reporter asked Bevo how he felt, he said, "I scored the points. I saw the ball go through. No matter what they do they can't hide what happened."

A few days later, Davis received a letter from Bland L. Stradley, chairman of the inspection committee of the Ohio College Association and an Ohio State vice president. He recommended that Davis limit Rio Grande's 1953 - 54 basketball schedule to a maximum of 25 games, to be played between December 1 and March 15. He warned that the good name of Rio Grande was at stake and that Oliver was an opportunist. Davis not only accepted the suggestions, but authorized Dean Lewis to consult with Stradley for confirmation and approval of Oliver's 1953 - 54 schedule. Moreover, he ordered the coach to submit requests for purchases, however minor, for approval by the Athletic Council. Oliver, reined in by the administration, accepted the new regulations and a token salary increase. But there was no way Newt Oliver was going to let Charlie Davis, Dean Lewis, and a few college trustees block the goals he had set for Bevo, the team, and himself.

Driven since youth by an insatiable desire for notoriety and the money he knew would follow, Oliver was an aggressive promoter and operator. As he led Bevo Francis into sports fame, he staked out a position that enabled him to achieve his goals. An archetype of the American way up, Oliver was a shrewd, canny entrepreneur, certain that the rules of academic tradition were no match for his vitality, charisma, and ability to flimflam Charlie Davis and the media. He knew that his 1953 contract was solid and that Bevo's high visibility would open up next year's schedule to big-name schools. And Oliver believed that if the college were saved, it would not be through God's efforts, but through his and Bevo's.

The coming of spring brought out the blazing red buds that blossomed on high banks north of Allen House. As the sounds of softballs slapping into worn leather gloves echoed against Anniversary Hall, men and women on dates and gangs of leftover friends checked out the scenes. As the days got longer, they piled into one or more of the few cars available and headed south to Cora Dam, the site of an ancient gristmill. There was water there, parking space, and a woods nearby that offered privacy for beer drinking and opportunities for coeds and their dates to hook up. Bevo, Wiseman, and McKenzie and others often cruised into Gallipolis, perhaps stopping first at Nate Morehouse's beer joint in Addison where a cold bottle of Burger beer sold for a quarter. In town at Gilkey's Queen Bee, the All-American Tavern served drinkers and an adjacent restaurant catered to those who just wanted to get a hamburger and listen to the sounds of steel balls hammering against bumpers on pinball machines. Up the river

Larry Varney collection

*Night club acts such as the one above played live music in bars near Rio Grand College in Gallia County, Ohio, where Bevo Francis and other students hung out. You could get cocktails there, as well as long neck bottles of Burger Beer. Larry Varney, center.*

on Route 7, three roadhouses, politely called night clubs, catered to the young and adventurous. The 7-35 Club, with live hillbilly music on weekends, attracted a working class crowd who came to drink, fight, and pick up girls. The Flamingo Club and the Blue Willow, further up the road at Kanauga, were less rowdy, but the beer and seven-sevens flowed freely. Ballplayers and other students danced both fast and intimate on the rosin-sprinkled dance floors in these places to the sounds of Les Paul's reverberating guitar in *Bye Bye Blues* long into the morning hours. In downtown Gallipolis, students with more money and those dressed up with dates were likely to stop after the movies at the Lafayette Bar and Grille located in the best hotel in town. A black bartender named Henry Doss, resplendent in white linen, served up Singapore Slings in a stylish manner. Boys without dates loafed at the Eagle's Club or the smoke-filled B and B Billiard Academy on Second Street where Bevo Francis, cigarette dangling from his lips, spent many hours playing nine-ball for a quarter a game. Ministerial students were content with the pristine activities of the College Christian Association with Dean Lewis's blessing.

Newt Oliver spent most of the summer of 1953 in the cramped, hot athletic office in Community Hall, connected by telephone to coaches' offices across the country. His efforts to schedule Yale University and Ohio State University, teams whose coaches had joined the attack on Bevo's records, were unsuccessful. But a number of large schools signed on. Villanova, Providence, Miami of Florida, North Carolina State, Wake Forest, Butler, Creighton, and Southeast Louisiana highlighted the schedule, no part of which would be played in the Hog Pen. Oliver, making the best of the situation, ordered new uniforms, several new balls, including a white one for warmups, and made airline reservations.

After a tranquil summer, school opened for the fall term, and again Bevo Francis, Newt Oliver, and Rio Grande College were drawing attention. James A. Rhodes, Republican candidate for governor, sought an endorsement from Oliver and Bevo. Oliver refused to get into that kind of politics, but in a whimsical move, he got Bevo elected constable of Raccoon Township. The story appeared in newspapers across the country, and Bevo's wife, Mary Jean, posed for a magazine that labeled her the "Pistol Packing Mama," taken from the title of a popular song.

These were typical of the media events that Bevo Francis was easily lured into by Oliver and accommodating reporters. With the exception of an occasional temperamental flare-up against Oliver and at having to be talked into television interviews by teammate Wayne Wiseman, Bevo was a humble, Appalachian kid who did what he was told to do by his coach. He followed the simple mores of his parents and his native hill country that included keeping one's word and honoring those who were in authority. Oliver had brought him from obscurity; he would be taken care of. So when Oliver played up Bevo's farm boy image with inventive stories of slopping hogs, and when photographers posed him in goofy situations, he played their game without hesitation. Bevo's physical size and athletic prowess overwhelmed reporters and fans, but he played the role of acolyte to his coach. His docile nature, which endeared him to others, prevented him from seizing opportunities. When the lights in the basketball arenas went up and the whistle blew for a jump-ball, he was like a tiger unleashed; but he found out later that ruthlessness reigned in the world of college and professional sports.

During the Thanksgiving holiday, the Redmen flew to Buffalo, Don Allen's hometown, to play Erie Tech. Allen was pleased to be among the 5,500 people who saw Rio Grande draw blood with 120 points to Erie's 59. The team's next foray was another air trip east that included stops at Madison Square Garden, the Philadelphia Arena, and the Boston Garden. When they arrived in New York City, Bevo was barraged by reporters and newscasters. On the day prior to his Garden appearance against Adelphi, he did six radio and television appearances beginning at 4:30 a.m. Joey Goldstein, the Garden's representative, orchestrated the day's events that culminated in a fashionable

French restaurant. Bevo, country as usual, passed up the frog legs rissole Provencale and ordered a medium rare sirloin. For dessert, without even looking at the carte du jour, he ordered jello and whipped cream. Oliver's order: "Make that two."

The following night, before a crowd of 14,000, Rio Grande choked as Adelphi beat them, 83 to 76. After 40 wins the Redmen's streak was over, and Jimmie Breslin wrote that "Their humiliating scores against nonentities is a travesty on the entire structure of intercollegiate athletics." Oliver and the team took a night of restless sleep and moved on to play the Villanova Wildcats. The lead switched back and forth 17 times; Bevo's 18-footer forced a tie at the end of regulation. In overtime, Villanova won, 92 to 91. Bob Vetrone wrote that "During the game there was almost a continual chant: 'Let's go Bevo,' and this from the supposedly tough Philly fans." The Redmen moved on to Boston Garden the next night and defeated Providence College, 89 to 87. Bob Cousy, among the crowd who saw Bevo, said, "What a wonderful touch that fellow has." When the team returned to campus, Oliver handed over $10,000 to President Davis. After two easy wins over minor opposition and with the holidays approaching, the team took its southern trip and defeated the University of Miami by 10 points. On the way home, they lost to North Carolina State, but came back the next night and defeated Wake Forest. Journalists continued to follow Bevo and the Redmen. *Newsweek* and *Real* magazine did feature stories. Dave Garroway's crew returned to campus to film another episode for national television. A polio benefit game played in Dayton against Findlay College brought $44,000 to charity and $4,000 to Rio Grande. But the publicity that Oliver cultivated continued to deepen the chasm between him and the college administration. Bevo was also frustrated by the attention and chuckled in the background as Oliver told reporters they couldn't see him because he'd gone back home to sell a hog.

On February 2 the Redmen played their 19th official game of the season. They had won 14 games and lost four. Although their record was not as dramatic as the year before, the elimination of play against two-year schools had not seriously damaged their game. And once again, Bevo had that one sizzling night. Michigan's Hillsdale College played Rio Grande at Jackson, Ohio, and in the 134 to 91 rout, Bevo scored 113, just three short of his 1953 record that was denied. The Basketball Hall of Fame requested the game ball and the score sheet. The rest of the 1954 season brought mixed results and ended with 20 wins and seven losses. Bevo's points for the year were 1,255, and his average per game was 46.5. When the Associated Press chose their All-Americans for 1954, Bevo was popular with the voters but had to settle for second-team honors. He was an easy choice for the NAIA's first team. In two seasons, the Redmen had won 61 games and lost seven. They played before 244,000 people and averaged 96.9 points per game. Attendance for single games varied from 13,000 at Madison Square Garden to 62 at the Hog Pen. Gate receipts ranged from $19.20 to $34,500.

By the first of April, rumors about Oliver and Bevo swirled around the college campus and in the media. Bevo was barely getting by. Little money, bad grades. Oliver was quoted: "If there are greener pastures we're ready to graze." After talks with Dean Lewis, the Athletic Council, and disgruntled faculty members, Davis finally decided to come down on the side of tradition. He asked Oliver to resign and threatened him with a charge of insubordination. Oliver stood on his three-year contract and told Davis he would stay as long as Don Allen stayed with him. Allen refused to get involved. A few days later bold headlines from the AP read: "Bevo Francis expelled for scholastic reasons." Bevo was charged with too many class cuts and failure to make up exams. The real story was that Oliver just drifted away with no formal paperwork and Bevo did go through the withdrawal process and his grades were good enough to stay in school, barely. He was above the 1.5 grade point average required for academic probation.

But Oliver, as usual, had a hole card to show. He knew there was money in professional basketball, that star players, especially those who could bring along their coach, were in demand. Bypassing the idea of forming his own barnstorming unit and an offer in public relations from Don Allen Chevrolet, he contacted Abe Saperstein of the Harlem Globetrotters. Oliver knew Saperstein was interested in Bevo's drawing power, that his organization was freewheeling, and that he could make a deal for both of them. After a few phone calls, Saperstein invited him and Bevo to New York City and on April 26 reported that the duo from Rio Grande had signed a one-year contract for $20,000 and expenses. In a dramatic gesture at a press conference, Saperstein presented Oliver and Bevo a bushel basket containing $4,000 in one-dollar bills. The Boston Whirlwinds, Saperstein's traveling foil to the Globetrotters, who always lost, had a new star player and coach.

The Globetrotter circuit took Oliver and Bevo on a grueling tour across the country, playing up to eight games a week. Summer games were often played on portable basketball floors in lighted ball parks. The 152 games scheduled for the winter season were played in facilities ranging from high school gyms to giant arenas in large cities. Leaving their families behind in Ohio, except for Christmas and spring breaks, Bevo, Oliver, and the rest of the entourage moved across the United States, from one city to another, to one hotel and then the next. When a reporter asked Bevo about professional basketball he said, "I went with my coach. But I miss my family. It's rough being away from home." Although he was a superior athlete, much of his reputation was built on hype generated by Oliver and media personnel eager to create a legend. Bevo loved basketball, but he hated the public adulation and the demand for press interviews in which he was often portrayed as a buffoon. But the money was coming in, and, with no college degree and no capacity to exploit his name and skills for himself, his opportunities were limited. Underlying these problems, and perhaps enhancing them, was his overwhelming desire to return to Wellsville, get back with his family and friends, and get out of the limelight forever. But Bevo and Oliver did sign on for a second season with a substantial pay raise. Oliver gave up his coaching job

and, traveling ahead of the teams, took charge of publicity and pro-
motion. No longer with Bevo on a daily schedule, the estrangement
between them, which had begun the year before, intensified as they
completed their second year. So after four years, with few vacations
from each other and tired of the road, they left the circuit and in separate directions.

Newt Oliver became a teacher and athletic director at Northwest-
ern High School in Springfield, Ohio, opened a Frosttop drive-in restaurant, and served two terms as Clark County Commissioner. The
frugal, flamboyant Oliver lectured throughout the United States on
Bevo's exploits, wrote a book, traded stocks, and farmed trees. A few
years after leaving Rio Grande, he made an uneasy peace with the
new administration and joined the college's board of directors in a
position with little influence. Today, Oliver still attends the annual
Bevo Francis Basketball Classic tournament, gives trophies to outstanding athletes, and his will calls for $1,000 for each man who
played for him still living when he dies. The friction that existed between him and Bevo has mellowed by time, and they see each other
at least once a year on the Rio Grande campus. Their story has been
sold to the Disney corporation.

Bevo continued to play semiprofessional ball. He barnstormed with
his own team, played in the Eastern League, and spent a year with the
Cleveland Pipers. In 1962, at the age of 30, disillusioned by team owners giving no-cut contracts to rookies, overweight and homesick, Bevo
retired and went home to Highlandtown. He settled in with his family and over the years worked in steel mills, heavy construction, and
trucking. He, too, has a friendly relationship with Rio Grande and
returns annually as a guest at the Bevo Classic. Bevo's number, 32,
was retired several years ago, and in 1986 the school gave him an honorary degree and inducted him into the Tau Kappa Epsilon fraternity.
His granddaughter played basketball at Rio Grande on a scholarship
in the 1990s. Leisure time takes him back to the woods for camping
and hunting, often with his wife, son Frank, daughter Marge, and his

three grandchildren. Content to sit in his living room with a cup of coffee and a cigarette, he turns down offers to speak. Although he keeps his trophies out of sight, his records are legendary. The NCAA, under division 11, gives him most points in a game, best season average, most field goals, and most attempts in a game. The NAIA adds to these records most free throws made and most attempted. Neither organization accepts the 116-point game that Rick Reilly called "the most mind numbing collaboration of boy and basketball in hoop history."

Young athletes in the area and at Rio Grande are inspired by his history and presence. Bevo Francis, in spite of the controversy and ballyhoo, lived and played straight in the best traditions of his Appalachian heritage. Charles Davis, who once denied him a small loan for groceries, left Rio Grande in 1954 for a school superintendent's job in Virginia and died at 61. Don Allen, who bought Bevo his first good suit of clothes, continued his financial support of the college, now called the University of Rio Grande, until his death at 58.

# Clyde Raymond Beatty
# Bainbridge Ohio's Cat Man

The happy riffs of *The Entry of the Gladiator* passed. The clowns and the girls in yellow tights faded into the background. Five-thousand people packed into the Hippodrome theater in New York City waited. The curtain over the 32-feet-wide steel cage rose. Artificial lightning and thunder flashed and boomed as the house lights went down. Tangled together, the aromas of cigarette smoke, popcorn, grease, and stale urine clinging to animal fur filled the room. Drums roared and the "...most dangerous, suicidal, blood-curdling wild animal display ever conceived by man" was on. A big African lion entered the cage and took his place atop a pedestal. More lions followed. A dozen tigers, possibly from Sumatra, came in, some taking places, others milling about. The trainer, resplendent in white cotton shirt and jodhpur pants, wide belt, and leather boots, jumped into the cage. He held a steel reinforced chair and a pistol loaded with blanks in his left hand, a rattan whip in his right. "Hup, hup," he yelled, moving fast around the cage, spotlight following. A lion lunged. The trainer cracked his whip, shoved his chair into the lion's face, and looked him in the eyes. The lion slapped the chair away. A moment later the cat was rolling over and over on the sawdust floor cued by a whip tickling its whiskers. The trainer's stance, props, body movements from his 145-pound frame, and cold eyes holding firm until the cat in his stare looked away, kept him in charge. He directed the 40 cats back to their pedestals and, leaning backward, signaled the center lion to stand on its hind legs. The finale came after 20 minutes of tense fury with the trainer,

Duane Null collection

*Three ladies on a summer outing in a horse-drawn buggy, Lawrence County, Ohio.*

drenched with sweat, working his way to the escape door. One cat missed the exit tunnel and circled him as he threw his props in the sawdust. Just as he slammed the cage door behind him, a lion slammed into it and the crowd rose to its feet. Clyde Raymond Beatty, *The Greatest Wild Animal Trainer of All Time*, from the village of Bainbridge, Ohio, had finished another day's work. After the show, he may have had a sandwich, a beer, and played some poker. He may have visited with Ernest Hemingway, Jack Dempsey, Grantland Rice, Lowell Thomas, or Mark Hellinger. His contract called for $70,000 for the run. At 34, he had risen from a poor Appalachian family to become the premier circus act in the western world, a celebrity wherever he went, a *Time* magazine cover story.

Clyde Beatty grew up in the Paint Creek Valley in Ross County, Ohio, just inside a section of the Appalachian Plateau. The creek, on its way to the Scioto River, runs through wide bottoms and rugged hills. Clyde was born there in 1903 to a lady named Margaret Everhart, a single mother. His father's name was James Edward Beatty. Growing up, he learned the lessons taught by hard times. Trapping muskrats, shooting squirrels, and catching fish, he helped his family get by and became forever attracted to the wildlife and the outdoors. He walked the dusty streets of Bainbridge barefoot in the summers passing newspapers. Clyde attended Bainbridge School and, if he had the money, took in silent flicks at the Pastime Theater. He was a good student who learned quickly and caused no trouble. The Beattys were poor, and by 1916, four girls and another boy were in the family. He and his half-sisters caught garter snakes and kept a menagerie of cats, dogs, and guinea pigs. Clyde picked up the nickname "Buster" as he grew into his teen years, and about 1920 he and some friends pooled their money and went, most likely, up to Washington Court House, about 30 miles west of Chillicothe, to take in Howes Great London Circus. Traveling shows were always looking for helpers, strong men and boys who could guide large animals from place to place, clean cages, carry water, and afford to work cheap, sometimes just for bed and board. When Howes left town Clyde was on the train. Although he came back from time to time to visit his mother and friends and spoke with fondness of his early years, the rest of his life was given over to romance, adventure, travel, and celebrity. He left behind poverty, his mother, the provincialism of a small town, his friends, and, perhaps, a teen-age love affair gone bad. He could not have chosen a better time.

For centuries long past, the kings and queens of Europe, Asia, and Africa had their personal jesters and mimes. Poor people tramped into the Circus Maximus in Rome to see gladiators and lions in gruesome spectacles of slaughter. During the Middle Ages every bazaar had its jugglers, acrobats, and snake charmers. The modern circus originated in England in the late eighteenth century and came to the United States before the century turned. Organized performers bought horses and wagons and took their acts to larger venues on outdoor stages and tents set up on grassy fields. No form of entertainment was more suited to this audacious land. The braggadocio and bravado of aerialists, clowns, and trained animals complemented the martial music, hustlers, and freaks in side shows. There was entertainment for all: young and old, rich and poor, in wheelchairs or on crutches, folks from group homes who had to be looked after, and people of all races and religions. Circus wagons pulled by horses moved westward as soon as settlements became big enough to accommodate them. The performers with European, Asian, and African origins were especially welcome in the big cities. When summers came, cold, dreary winters over, traveling shows were natural extensions of church dinners, picnics, boat rides, family reunions, county fairs, and ethnic celebrations. George Washington gave his blessings. Abraham Lincoln and Zachary Taylor were entertained by a clown named Dan Rice. Buffalo Bill and Theodore Roosevelt were friends. What could be more entertaining than the sideshow barker snapping into a cheap microphone "Come on in...for one thin dime...see our Brazilian senorita. She shimmies, she shakes, she wriggles on her belly like a reptile," or announcing the Ubangi Savages from Congo "...with mouths and lips as large as crocodiles"? Human cannonballs, tattooed ladies, hermaphrodites, and, yes, dog-and-pony shows, moved westward on horse-drawn wagons. And there was Terrell Jacobs, "...trainer of ferocious killers of the jungle, hitherto untamable and unconquerable."

In the late 19th century, traveling by train, shows were performed in large tents with three rings of action going on at the same time. As the 20th century and the industrial age came around, more people, better roads, and good times brought mixed news to circus owners and performers. Movies, vaudeville shows, amusement parks, and easy travel from rural towns to big cities, left traditional circuses scrambling for bigger and better spectacles. Animals from the jungles had always been top attractions. Before zoos came, giraffes, elephants, tigers, lions, pumas, boa constrictors, and leopards were rare sights. But better than just letting folks look at animals in cages was the idea of a trainer engaging wild beasts in a show. J.A. Van Amburgh had entered cages with wild beasts as early as 1833 and is given the dubious credit of being the first man to put his head into a lion's mouth. He was a German and used a gentle style with lions presenting them as obedient and playful, their aggression suppressed. The Howes Great London Circus, Clyde Beatty's first gig, had a long history of animal shows with large groups of trained elephants as far back as 1874.

Clyde Beatty spent his first winter on the road in Montgomery, Alabama, feeding and watering animals, cleaning dung from lion cages, doing odd jobs, meeting a variety of performers, and learning the nomadic life of traveling shows. In 1922, the show began the season under the name of the Gollmar brothers and the next year moved to Peru, Indiana with John Robinson. Beatty practiced there with a polar bear act under the guidance of Peter Taylor and Jules Castane both of whom had worked with lions and tigers. Learning the ethos of circus life firsthand, and feeling confident that he could work his way into a prominent place, Beatty studied animal behavior from such works as Charles Darwin's *The Expressions of the Emotions in Man and Animals*. His intuition was that animals had emotions, individual traits, and character. Studying research and visiting zoological societies satisfied him that he was onto something. He learned to keep his animals well-fed, groomed, and healthy through regular visits by veterinarians. He learned what spooked them, how they communicated with one another, how males related to females, how they played, and what made them happy. Although the lion and tiger show that made him famous was aggressive, dangerous, and volatile, it was Beatty's ticket to stardom and it gave him a chance to bring out the ferocity, beauty, and intelligence of the jungle beasts. He liked his cats fresh from the jungles and, within the constraints of their lives in captivity, kept them pure. He trained them to submit to his commands using a limited amount of physical force and behaviorism—traditional carrot and stick techniques. However, he did pet his animals when they seemed to ask for it, used his whip to touch their whiskers in an affectionate manner, and returned to the cage after shows to show his appreciation. His life on the road with lions and tigers began in 1925 with the Hagenbeck-Wallace exposition. His first setback came a year later when a 500-pound lion attacked him during a performance and, as the crowd cheered thinking it was part of the act, Beatty had to be dragged out of the cage by a helper using an iron rake. Scrapes like this that were played up in newspapers and gossip among circus groups led to feature articles on him in *Field And Stream* and *The Literary Digest.*

By 1931, Clyde Beatty's act was so hot that he was able to get away from the big-top outdoor shows for a run in Madison Square Garden sponsored by Ringling Brothers-Barnum and Bailey, the so-called *Greatest Show on Earth.* Advance notices bragged about the return of ferocious beasts presented by a trainer risking maiming and death at each performance. Beatty did not let the New Yorkers down. His show received good reviews from critics who covered the performances, and the city was amenable to his midwestern, "Aw shucks" attitude. Critics talked about Beatty's nerve, showmanship, courage, and how he often came within 18 inches of jungle cats whose wide-open mouths snarled and dripped with saliva. Among the reporters was Edwin C. Hill, famous for the tag line "The human side of the news" on network radio. O.O. McIntyre of Gallipolis, Ohio, made a favorable reference to the show in his syndicated column which reached over 100 million readers. Two live radio shows were broadcast from the Garden featuring interviews with Frank Buck, Courtney Cooper, John Ringling, and Beatty. Among the guests with complimentary tickets on the show's last day were 15,000 orphans and handicapped children who were enthralled by Beatty's act.

In January of 1932, as national publications were beginning to offer features about Beatty and Metro-Goldwyn-Mayer movie studios had hired him to advise on the filming of a Tarzan movie, he broke the code of the veldt and turned his back on a lion. During a training session in Peru, Indiana, Nero caught him off guard, attacked, and sank a fang into his right thigh. Aides took Beatty to a local hospital where doctors cauterized the wound. When Beatty developed a high fever, they were suspicious of an infection from the lion's saliva and cut into the wound. The doctors found the infection, drained it, sewed up the leg and, with a few weeks convalescence, he was ready to take on New York again. Beatty's confrontation with Nero made big news on the radio and in the newspapers, some writers calling his illness "jungle fever." With the Great Depression on, and ominous rumbles of war coming from Europe and Asia, stories of the lion trainer's invincibility and daring offered many people a hero for the times. Beatty's second gig at the Garden in New York City, where he was billed over the Great Wallendas' death-defying aerial act, had been talked up for months by commentators like Walter Winchell and others among the city's literati. Beatty's act did not disappoint regular fans, the rich and famous in the good seats, or the press. Praise for the farm boy with dozens of cat scratch scars, his role in bringing John Ringling's show back to its prior glory, and his comparison in status to Jack Dempsey, Gene Tunney, Eddie Rickenbacker, and Babe Ruth were major themes. Occasional reports of violence seemed to enhance a legend in the making. Readers shrugged and Beatty was nonplussed when a newspaper writer told about an ugly incident in Cleveland's Public Hall. A 400-pound lion named Sammy, having killed a young female lion, was put into a cage with four lions during a training session. Beatty sicced the lions on Sammy and, as he cracked his whip, the lions attacked in a flurry of screeches and clawings. Sammy slunked to the wooden runway, presumably having learned his lesson.

Clyde Beatty grasped the opportunities. *American Magazine, Physical Culture, Literary Digest,* and *Colliers* did pieces on him, his show, his views on lions and tigers, and his flirtations with danger. Edward Anthony of *Colliers* helped him write a book, *The Big Cage,* which was later made as a movie by Universal Pictures with Beatty playing himself. A reviewer in the New York Times praised the star's enthusiasm, the film's realism, and its action scenes that took the audience beyond a weak plot. In 1934, he starred in a second film, *The Lost Jungle*, with Cecilia Parker and Mickey Rooney. Beatty's B movies made money, and he considered leaving the road and settling down in Hollywood full-time as a Ringling Brothers's boss grumbled that appearing in films diminished the value of his live show. But Beatty's metier was working shows on the road and basking in the attention offered by thrilled spectators. He gave up on the Ringling organization which owned part of the Hagenbeck-Wallace circus and was picked up by Jess Adkins and Zack Terrell in a new group called the Cole Brothers show, which soon added Beatty's name to the marque. The new show opened on schedule at the Chicago Coliseum on April 20, 1935. During downtime, while keeping up a busy traveling schedule, he went again to Hollywood for a new film, *The Lost Jungle*, which was pre-

*Clyde Beatty, circa 1932.*

June Gregg collection

sented as a serial. Two years later he starred in another serial called *Darkest Africa*. Caricatures of him and his trained lions also appeared in *Big Little Books* and *Popular Comics*. The Studebaker car company became a sponsor, gave him a new model called the President, and pictured him with the car in magazine advertisements. Beatty was also proud to endorse Ever Ready batteries, and Canadian Club whiskey. Even political cartoons suggested that Roosevelt's General Hugh Johnson, head of the National Recovery Act, could use some of Beatty's flair.

Clyde Beatty was intrinsically drawn to the circus and his animals. The books and articles he wrote in as-told-to form and the letters he sent to friends revealed a person whose purpose in life was to excel as a circus performer. He loved not only the training and care of lions and tigers, but also the rough-and-tumble life on the road, the interaction with fellow travelers, all-night poker games, and telling tales as the circus train rumbled from town to town, lions and tigers swaying from side to side in locked cages. Beatty enjoyed irony, and hardly a performance was given without a woman fainting, a clown getting too close to a lion, reporters asking stupid questions, and circus managers leaving worthless roustabouts behind in some strange town. Less often, he played veterinarian and pulled a lion's tooth or broke up a fight between two snarling tigers. He had a cross-eyed lion when he lived in Rochester, Indiana, named Leo, who had the run of the house. He used swats with a folded newspaper to housebreak Leo and taught him how to get a drink of water from a lavatory faucet. Beatty drove around towns in a convertible with two lion cubs in the front seat with him. And, surely for publicity, he got lucky thinking he owned five little lion sisters about the time the Dionne quintuplets of Canada were front-page news. When he, or someone, found out two of them were males, he stopped showing them around and inviting newspapers to take their pictures. He coped with lions breaking out and going downtown on the loose and with house lights going off, possibly on purpose, during night shows leaving him in a dark cage with a cache of wild animals and a house full of gasping men, women, and children. When the Erie County New York Society for the Prevention of Cruelty to Animals threatened to have Beatty arrested for the "uncalled for prodding and beating of lions and tigers", he invited their leader into the cage with him during his act. No one took him up on the challenge, but a newspaper writer said Beatty toned down his next performance. After one of his shows in Pittsburgh, two constables arrested him after a complaint from the local humane society. His accusers testified in court that Beatty fired blank shots into the animals' faces and used a "whip cracker" to agitate them. His response was that he was not dealing with dogs, he had to be firm, and if he were hurting the cats they would attack him. The judge fined him 20 dollars and costs. Beatty paid up and moved on to the next town. Circus owners and show names came and went, performers were ripped off, and disgruntled partners filed lawsuits; but Beatty was not a person to grovel, make excuses, or show self-pity. He enjoyed the company of the Giraffe-Neck women from Burma, billed as *The Greatest Educational Attraction The World Has Ever Known,* and joked about marrying at least one of them. Beatty traveled to Berlin, Germany, to see what a writer for the *Literary Digest* called a tigon, a cat produced in a zoo from a male tiger bred to a female lion. He was disappointed in the animal's looks and gave up on trying to put one into his circus. Beatty once shot himself in the leg with a wad from his blank pistol and, again, was hospitalized. Rich and famous, making $3,500 a week in season, he was the top attraction among the circuses in North America.

Clyde Beatty spent the summer of 1939 performing at the Million Dollar Pier in Atlantic City, New Jersey. During World War II, attendance and interest in circus acts began to diminish. Beatty hooked up with the Johnny Jones organization in the early forties where he carried his own act within the larger show. He operated a Jungle Zoo in Akron, Ohio, for a summer, established an animal farm in Fort Lauderdale, Florida, and coauthored another book, *Jungle Performers,* with

Earl Wilson. He continued to move about the country with both the Wallace and Russell Brothers troupes which traveled in trucks. In 1945 Beatty bought out the Russell brothers and formed his own circus and returned to the rails again, using 15 cars carrying as many as 500 people. He rode in a luxurious private coach with rattan furniture from Manila, paintings of jungle scenes, two bedrooms, a galley, and a bathroom. He held on through extensive travel expenses and a wreck in Nebraska that killed one person, injured several others, and damaged much of the show's equipment. Only one other railroad show was on the road instead of the 15 or more in the thirties, and the traditional circus parades through towns ended and became part of circus history.

Beatty returned to Hollywood in 1949 and was featured in a movie with Abbot and Costello called *Africa Screams.* He continued touring during the 1950s with his own show and starred in a radio program on the Mutual Network sponsored by the Kellogg Cereal Company. *Colliers* magazine reprised his 30 years on the road with a full-color feature, but attendance at shows continued to dwindle even as his bouts of mayhem with the cats continued. A lion killed two female tigers in Detroit, and he was mauled during a confrontation in Portland, Oregon. Once again Beatty returned to the movies. He played himself in a flick with Phyllis Coates called *Perils of the Jungle* and the next year, with John Wayne putting up some of the money, *Ring Of Fear,* featuring Mickey Spillane and Pat O'Brien was brought out by Warner Brothers. In 1956, his circus went broke and was bought out by two investors who took it to Deland, Florida, for the winter. Three years later, his name returned to the show as the Clyde Beatty-Cole Brothers circus. At the age of 59, Beatty, with the help of his assistant, Red Hartman, was still on the road. He did his familiar show in the Detroit Coliseum for the Shrine Circus in February, 1963. A writer for *Newsweek* reviewed the show and quoted Beatty in an after-show interview: "When I get 'em fresh from the jungle, they're afraid of me. As I work 'em they get used to me. And then they'll turn. Nine times

out of ten, a lion will kill a tiger in a fight. But the lion is more ferocious toward me. Lions bluff. When tigers come, they mean it." Beatty
hadn't changed, but the world had. Jack Parr, Ed Sullivan, and Mike
Wallace gave him television exposure in a new medium that was also
bringing authentic films on exotic animals in natural settings to its
audience. Colorful, inviting amusement parks with thrill rides drawing families, zoos changing their emphasis on caged animals to large
fenced areas with greenery, some now referring to jungles as rain forests, worries about rare animals dying out, anthropologists presenting papers showing that full lips on women are attractive to males in
many cultures, and the activities of animal rights activists left acts
like Beatty's on ever-shifting sand.

In the summer of 1964, with his third book, *Facing The Big Cats,*
coming out, Beatty began to lose energy and left Red Hartman to do
the show while he went to Chicago to see a doctor. He was operated
on and in early 1965 tried to work the show but, feeling ill and with
his doctor's advice, turned it over to Hartman and returned to his
home overlooking the Pacific Ocean in Ventura, California. There,
on July 19 in Community Memorial Hospital, he died from cancer at
the age of 61. Three days later, on a sunny Friday, six pallbearers carried his coffin into the Church of the Hills at Forest Lawn Memorial
Park in the Hollywood Hills for last rites. Movie actor Pat O'Brien delivered the eulogy, and popular author Mickey Spillane sat near the
family. The man who had entertained millions for 40 years; sustained
numerous maulings in front of crowds; played to audiences as large
as 103,000 at the Nebraska State Fair; performed in every major city
including Ottawa, Canada, Honolulu, Hawaii, and Mexico City; was
entombed in Forest Lawn Cemetery. His crypt, near the resting places
of Charles Laughton, Gene Autry, and Ricky Nelson, has a bas relief
of a lion etched into its granite facade. A few days later, Clyde Beatty
became the 49th performer elected to the Circus Hall Of Fame in
Sarasota, Florida.

# Revival

They came down the dirt road that ran along Greasy Ridge and the roads that snaked along the rich bottom land in the Indian Guyan valley. Some came in cars, rusted-out Plymouths and Chevrolets, and old Model A Fords churning up dust that settled on the ironweeds and daisies that grew along the ditches. Farmhands with sun-darkened skin and strong muscles bummed free rides on the running boards of cars, holding on with one arm stuck through the open windows holding on tight to the center post. Some came walking, groups of scrubbed boys and girls laughing and giggling, the younger kids running on ahead climbing over and under fences, skipping rocks across the green water that stood in pools in the creek bed. Roads and trails led to the white frame church that sat on a high knoll by a graveyard. This was Good Hope Baptist Church in Gallia County, Ohio. It was 1940.

The lonesome sound of a thousand June bugs rang out from the grove across the valley on that hot August night. The church bell keeper, a hunchback man dressed in bib overalls, paced up and down the gravel-covered church parking lot, chain-smoking Camels, a habit he picked up in Uncle Sam's Army in World War I. One by one, people stepped through the church doors and made their way up the aisles and sat down on the homemade wooden benches. The pale yellow light from six coal oil lamps that hung along the walls flickered on the scene. Millers, fat from summer feeding, buzzed on and off the lamps. As eight o'clock approached, a new black LaSalle coupe with an unspoiled layer of dust clinging to its shiny chrome and paint crunched through the gravel and stopped near the church doors. The preacher, Clifford Cremeans, had arrived.

Cremeans was a man of the Lord. Dressed in an off-white linen suit, he got out of his car, waved his Bible to onlookers and entered the church. His body movements and square hat exuded authority and respect, even from the drinkers and brawlers of the community. No one looked the preacher man in the eye that didn't look away first. He owned the night. And as he walked up the aisle to take a special chair beside the pulpit, the congregation, believers down front, sinners in the back, stood and sang:

> *Standing on the promises of Christ my King,*
> *Through eternal ages let His praises ring,*
> *Glory in the highest, I will shout and sing,*
> *Standing on the promises of God.*

Many did. In these hollows where coal banks spilled sulfur into the creeks and hillside flats had to be grubbed out for a few rows of tobacco, there wasn't much else to believe in. A doctor practiced two miles away at Crown City, but his knowledge was primitive. Roosevelt's New Deal had brought electric power through, but few had the money to buy radios, refrigerators, and washers. Everyone except the undertaker and a few grocers used outdoor toilets. Most young women married early and bore as many children as nature allowed. Fewer babies died than in the great influenza epidemic of 1918, but still they died. Down-and-out people were either taken in by families or they went to the poorhouse.

Most people had never traveled beyond local towns like Gallipolis and Ironton, let alone Columbus, Cincinnati, or Maysville, Kentucky, where cured tobacco was bought and sold. A few adventurous men did, however, join the Civilian Conservation Corps and wound up clearing roads in Nevada. Blacks and other ethnic groups, as well as Catholics, had settled in the cities leaving the hill land peoples white and Protestant. The only people who had gone beyond high school were schoolteachers, and they were locals gone off for a few semesters and returned with the same values they left with. Two or three men in the area had achieved some notoriety by doing time in the Big House. There was hope in fellowship and brotherhood, but this was based on following the Lord and keeping His commandments. There was no middle ground. No gray areas or moral relativity. One group was saved for eternity by coming forward, repenting, getting baptized, joining church, and staying out of trouble. The rest were lost. Old enough to know better, they drank, blackguarded, worked on Sunday, stole chickens, and fornicated. A major task for the saved was to bring this group of sinners into the fold, to show them how they too could look beyond the vale.

Most people came to the big meeting because they really believed there was a better world "over yonder," and only those who followed Jesus and lived right would ever see it. These included mothers who prayed and asked others to join them in asking the Lord to rescue sons who had grown up without accepting Christ and were lost. A few quiet skeptics came as their ancestors had for a hundred years. Being a good Christian was helpful socially and politically. The young ones came because their parents made them, and there wasn't much else to do except listen to Jack Benny on the radio or chase lightning bugs in the summer heat. Teenagers came to meet friends, to be with other boys and girls, to flirt, to make dates for future nights as the meeting continued, and walk home together. It wasn't unusual for a few new babies to arrive nine months later. But all who came had one thing in common: they were part of a community of human life struggling for existence and truth. As true believers prayed aloud in a united prayer, voices unspoiled by the wands of choir directors sang:

> *Just over in the glory land,*
> *I'll join the happy angels band,*
> *Just over in the glory land,*

*Just over in the glory land,*
*There with the mighty host I'll stand,*
*Just over in the glory land.*

Inside the church the air of dog days hung close to the floor. Old women fanned their faces with hand fans provided by the local undertaker. The varnished oak altar bench, polished up, sat in front of the pulpit ready to accommodate sinners who could be induced to come forward near the close of the service. An upright piano in the front corner rang softly with minor riffs at the hands of a teenage girl in a summer dress. Hardwood benches nearly filled with people stretched from the front of the church to the back. On the wall high behind the pulpit, a framed print of an unknown artist's rendering of Jesus of Nazareth, the popular Jesus with a bearded white face, looked down on the stark accouterments and plain people. Near the picture on the wall a sign board told how much money was given and how many came last Sunday morning. As the girl at the piano sounded a mighty chord in 4/4 time, once again the simple sounds of country faith came forth.

Paula Newsome collection

*Unknown West Virginia lady dressed for church.*

*Where He leads me I will follow,*
*Where He leads me I will follow,*
*Where He leads me I will follow,*
*I'll go with Him, with Him, all the way.*

Preacher Cremeans took over the service from a lay leader, put on his glasses, and read selected verses from the Bible. Then he closed the book and spoke without notes, strictly from the spirit—wherever it took him. Now God himself was putting words in his mouth, telling him what to say. He took off his jacket and threw it to the side, men and women near him shouting, "Amen, amen." He walked back and forth behind the pulpit calling out, "Hey, how many of you love the Lord, huh; you know this could be our last day on God's green earth, huh; what would happen to you tonight if the clouds broke apart and Jesus came here to this ridge, huh; this could be your last day on earth, the day you will die." Sweat came and he wiped his face with a handkerchief. He told them how his life used to belong to the Devil. How he used to guzzle beer in the beer joints in Huntington, get into fist fights, pick up women, sometimes spend the night in jail. But the Lord with his grace had saved him from all that. Now he had a wonderful wife and lovely children. Since the night he was converted—lust, greed, and other sins the Devil threw in his face had been taken care of by the blood of Jesus. And praise God for it. He went on, slower now and looking into the eyes of sinners in the back, trying to make them squirm. He told them of a dream he had had many times. He sat in the shade of a big maple tree that stood near the creek bank where the water was still and deep. It was deep summer and a breeze redolent of honeysuckles and bluebells swirled about. His loved ones were there. His mother holding a dish of potato salad. His father sitting on the running board of a Model T Ford. Grandpa and Grandma, brothers and sisters talking and laughing gaily. But when he awoke, many of them were gone. Long since dead and lying in graves dug in the poor dirt of Guyan Township. His own fate written in the wind.

He paused, and the church was silent. He stepped down now stand-ing closer to his people, many mesmerized by his words, gestures, and tears.

The eyes of the faithful stayed on the preacher. Sinners finally looked up. Women fanned and men removed their wool suit jackets. Babies who had cried off and on, even one or two who had been slapped in the face by their mothers, were stretched out asleep among adults and older brothers and sisters on the benches. Hardened sin-ners eased out of their seats and out the door, every remaining head turning to see who was leaving. The preacher, exhausted and hoarse, gave the altar call and the crescendo of emotion wilted as the crowd stood and sang:

> *Oh, why not tonight?*
> *Oh, why not tonight?*
> *Wilt thou be saved?*
> *Then why not tonight?*

As the soft, sweet singing continued, Cremeans begged the sinners in the back rows to come forward and seek forgiveness for their sins. He asked them to seek salvation, to come and pray at the altar. Back-sliders and new mourners alike. A woman told a reluctant man in his late twenties that his dead mother in heaven would never see him again unless he was saved. He told her to get the hell away from him and ran out the door. The woman understood. The Devil had a hold of that man. A young man left the comfort of his seat in the back corner and made his way forward up the center aisle. When he reached the pulpit area, he sank to his knees and placed his head on his folded arms on the altar bench. The singing continued, lower now, and the preacher joined true believers in loud praying for the man's soul, ask-ing the Lord to bring him through. They prayed, loud and long in choral tones rising from their knees one by one as their voices gradu-ally became still. The man, his eyes wet with emotion, pushed himself to his feet and stood facing the others. The preacher and the church members fell in line, passing by to shake his hand, offer congratulations, and, sometimes, hug him, saying, "amen, amen." As the line moved forward, everyone now shaking with everyone else, they sang that ancient piece that transcends cultures and dogma:

> *Amazing Grace, how sweet the sound,*
> *That saved a wretch like me.*
> *I once was lost, but now am found,*
> *Was blind, but now I see.*

In groups of threes and fours, they headed toward the rear of the church, gathering together in families and groups much as they had come. They visited leisurely with friends and acquaintances as they left the church, absorbing the sultry heat that darkness had failed to diminish. Many who had walked took rides home in cars. Most would be back tomorrow night, even though the men faced a ten-hour day in the yellow tobacco fields and the women must peel and cook

Lavette Compton collection

*Jesus tree, southern West Virginia.*

Duane Null collection

*Sandfork Creek, near Lecta, Ohio, circa 1920. Water baptizing was an essential part of most rural churches in Appalachia. The success of summer revivals and tent meetings by itinerant preachers was measured by the number of folks who accepted Jesus Christ as their Savior and submitted to the ritual of having their bodies immersed in a local creek or river.*

peaches for putting up in glass jars. The sinners would even come back, although they knew they would again face the preacher's chastisement. This was the last great get-together until the fall when Mercerville School would sponsor a pie supper or a Halloween carnival. As the preacher eased the big, white steering wheel on his LaSalle coupe to the left and passed out of everyone's sight, he pushed in the cigarette lighter and shook a fresh Lucky Strike from its crisp, green package, and lit up. Walter Winchell was ending his radio newscast out of New York, warning of a big war across the waters. Here on Greasy Ridge, the September rain would end the sludge of dog days and, who knew, maybe a dozen new converts would be candidates for baptizing in a deep pool in Indian Guyan Creek.

# Foggy Riffs

I'm not saying my family was poor, but I remember reading news-papers that had been used as wallpaper. Read them right on the wall. Good stuff, but sometimes you had to stand on your head. A little out-of-date, but the stories were there for me to look over while the older folks were out in the fields. Headlines of great stories like Hitler's move across Europe, Roosevelt's plan to feed the hungry, the missing Lindbergh baby, Father Divine's Rolls Royce, and Hollywood's queen, Rita Hayworth. Who could enjoy life without this kind of knowledge? No, really, we had other reading material: hubcaps, grocery products, Sears-Roebuck catalogs, tombstones, household appliances, Big Little books with flashing movies built in, Action comics, and when forced under threat of having to bury a maggot-infested dead animal, Bible verses. "Jesus wept," was my personal favorite. When I refused to memorize my weekly Bible verse, Dad made me listen to Edwin C. Hill give what he called the human side of the news on the radio. Even in the summer when you got nothing but static. Was this small and petty? I reckon not. My grandpa John was a piece of work. He taught me to read whiskey labels when I was five. He would hold up a half-empty fifth and say, "Now what's that say?" I'd say, "Looks like Jim Beam to me, Grandpa." Then he'd grin and say, "Don't tell your Mom." Grandpa never paid any attention to the legal season for trap-ping. When it got cold and the fur was right for winter, he'd get out there on the creek banks and set steel traps. I looked in his deepfreeze one day and he had two quarts of vanilla ice cream, a side of beef, 10 packages of Birds-Eye frozen corn, and three minks. He was in his eighties and had never washed his hair. I think he went into Guyan

Creek a couple times every summer and bathed with homemade soap.

About 1943, in the middle of World War II, things got better. They did. Now I don't mean to say we were bootlegging sugar ration stamps or gouging Uncle Sam on scrap iron. With the boys across the waters sleeping in cold mud and snow, dodging Hitler's 88 millimeters, and drinking beer in French cabarets, money began to flow down better. Prices for the milk Dad sold went up, tobacco was guaranteed to bring a good price or the friendly government man would buy it himself. Still we had not been weaned from those old McGuffey readers. If they were good enough for Mom and Dad, brothers and sisters, they must have some life left in them. They smelled old, like an attic, or a piece of furniture from Thomas Edison's workshop. When the binding came apart, my Mom sewed it back on with needle and thread. My sister kept saying, "We're throwing them durn things out, I'm sick of looking at them." Mom's going, "No way you're throwing them out, there's stuff in them to teach you morals. And you all could use some." Never

*The author's birthplace on Williams Creek, Gallia County, Ohio. The bottom behind the barn was used for tobacco farming. Four children were raised here on 100 acres of hill and bottom land. One child was buried in the Crown City graveyard.*

Author's collection

mind that the McGuffeys were void of irony with enough morbid poems and essays to break the average child. My oldest brother wrote in one: "When this you see remember me/Although on earth I may not be/And if the grave should be my bed/Remember me when I am dead." Pleasant thought for a 10-year-old. And complementing that was the bedtime prayer: "Now I lay me down to sleep/I pray the Lord my soul to keep/If I should die before I wake/I pray the Lord my soul to take." Is that a good thing to say to a child? "Remember, you might die in the night." But sometimes the doggerel got a bit more positive: "I do believe the God above/Created you for me to love." Pickup line from the 1920s. How about this one: "Sugar is sweet/Butter is greasy/I love you/Don't be uneasy." But when I got too melancholy I pulled out my Big Little Books. Each page had a drawing in the upper right corner, and when you flipped them fast they told a story in moving pictures. I had seen maybe one or two movies on the screen in Gallipolis.

My sister lived in town and she used to bring magazines and Sunday comics out. She had better stuff than the *Ohio Farmer* my Dad took. *Life, Look,* and the ever-popular *Saturday Evening Post.* These magazines had good pictures: dead Americans lying in the sand on Omaha Beach, socialites like Wallace Warfield Simpson, airplanes, fat people, and three-headed calves. And the advertisements were even better: Kelvinator refrigerators with smiling housewives standing next to them, new Buicks with grills seven-feet tall, shampoos for beautiful hair, and suits from Palm Beach. Like Dad was going to get a summer suit and march in the Easter parade. Even if Dad was in the Easter parade he'd wear a dark wool suit and high-top dress shoes. He was a 19th-century person. His given name was Grover, my mother's was Flossie. Worse yet, they were cousins, both named Fulks, a word few can pronounce and none can spell. My parents finally bought a few books: *A Child's Garden of Verses,* by Robert Stevenson, had poems a child could have read to him over and over. "The Land of Counterpane" and "My Shadow" are two I remember. We also had *Treasure Island,* a book I came to like. "Yo, ho, ho, and a bottle of rum." There were several rum-drinking pirates on Greasy Ridge. On those rare Saturdays when we went into town, I found Fontana's Market where you could buy candied cherries, ice cream, hot dogs, and comic books such as Superman, Batman, and Dick Tracy. From these sources for words, phrases, and stories, I got into the habit of reading. I even liked to read poetry but never let on. I found that reading was a way to combat loneliness and to pass time. I read in cars, on school busses, in the barn, and under shade trees. Then came junior high school at dear old Mercerville.

The six years between seventh grade and graduation from high school put me in touch with a few books, newspapers, and magazines. It did take me a while to figure out why girls liked athletes better than bookish wimps; after I studied biology and anthropology and gained some worldly experience, however, I finally rose to be at least a dork. Textbooks, however boring and filled with propaganda, were of some value, and the small library had a few new periodicals we could read in study hall. Miss McClure, the English teacher, thought if she made us study works like *Ivanhoe*, we would attain high culture. Come on. After high school and one semester of college, I joined the Air Force. Truman said we had to fight those Communists, weird people who might as well have been Dixiecrats as far as I was concerned. You know about how much a rural high school in southern Ohio would open a student's world to Karl Marx. The teachers there had trouble identifying Groucho Marx. I just thought it would be good to avoid the draft and get my choice of branches. Traveling around the world at age 19 still on the lookout for something to read, among more devious interests. I had a few bucks and, like a magnet, was drawn to newsstands in cities and railroad stations. Sitting on my bunk in an open-bay barracks in Tucson, Arizona, however, brought the melancholia out as it would to most Appalachians who can leave home physically but not mentally. I was not only two days from home, but surrounded by the color brown, cactuses, and tarantulas as big as rabbits. And heat that made car radiators boil over just sitting at a red light. As an enlisted man, I had decent work as an aircraft mechanic, good buddies, time to drink, smoke, and look for girls. Them Pall Malls was good. Otherwise, I continued to read. One time in the heat of a Texas August, I hitchhiked to the state fair in Dallas. After a day on the Ferris wheel and watching the serpent woman shimmy and shake, I walked into a bookstore and put down three dollars of my own money for a copy of James Jones' *From Here to Eternity*. I had read reviews of the book and knew it was a story about the Army before WWII and that it was a no-holds-barred account of the lives of a bunch of ragtag enlisted men and officers seeking advancements before the war came. First time I had ever bought a hardback book. *Eternity* was true to the way I had seen the world work, clear with strong nouns and verbs, and got it done showing how the military class system works. Officers, college graduates all, had better billets, earned more money, loafed with high-class girls at the officers' clubs. And we had to salute them and take orders, obey that sacred chain of command. I was living and learning something I had suspected all along: rich people live better than poor people.

After an undistinguished stint in the Air Force, I spent my rocking chair money and went back to college. I was thinking I might as well use up the government money I was eligible for and get me a job teaching school down at Mercerville. They used to say, "He got hisself a school." I taught there and worked as a principal for a few years while continuing to work on gradu-

The author, Airman Second Class, United States Air Force, Strategic Air Command, circa 1953.

Author's collection

ate courses at Marshall University. Finally I got a master's degree and, with some government money left, had nowhere else to go but work on a doctor's degree. I didn't know what that was but it sounded good. So I got me a new Ford on the installment plan and headed south to Knoxville. Next thing you know, running between Knoxville and Columbus where I worked at my second job in school administration, I could see myself as a college professor. "Are you serious?" my young wife went, feeding a six-month-old girl. "You couldn't teach the third grade."

I took a teaching job at Marshall University in the College of Education and moved my family to Huntington, West Virginia. My wife said she had seen a lot of hick towns but this one took the cake. Throw in a couple of slices of Jim's banana pie. Said she would rather move back to Bullskin, a suburb of Mercerville. Columbus had a shopping center and a zoo. Huntington had an old cafeteria and a craft show once a year. Sandra would have left then, as she did later, if she had any place to go. We had two girls, one in school, one at home and I was trying to get my wife interested in the faculty wives' club. After doing all that reading, research, and writing a doctoral dissertation, I thought I might as well try to write a few things for publication. The administrators liked that. So I learned a lot of big words. It was nothing for me to use words like, "cognitive," "imbroglio," "apperceptive," and phrases like, "congruence of perception." My personal favorite was a word I worked into conversations and lectures as often as I could: "oeuvre." One day after class a pretty girl from Boone County, West Virginia, and I've yet to see an ugly girl from that county, came up and said, "Hey, Dr. Fulks?" "What's that?" I say. She goes, "No one knows what the hell you're talking about." I just said, "Oh." Then I quit reading and started writing. I sent some essays off. Some reported research and opinions in the field of education. If they didn't have big words and could be understood, they were returned from editors with regrets. Regrets? Please. Others were stories about life in Appalachia. If they didn't have small, simple words and sentences, they came

Dale Holschuh collection

*Scottown school, 1940. Chet Murdock, the teacher, far right.*

back. Now my Mom didn't raise no foolish children, you see what I'm saying? If you are ever going to sell a story you are going to have to learn to write so it is interesting and people can understand what you are talking about.

Working on my writing skills, I began thinking that my three college degrees were keeping me from selling stories. I knew too many big words and had forgotten the little ones I learned back home. It seemed to follow that what I had to work into my essays were the language, life, times, values, and culture of my native land. Forget some of the college stuff and use the words you heard the day laborers in the tobacco fields use. This idea led me to propose at Marshall that we offer a program to take away earned degrees and turn graduates back into normal people. The administration didn't go for it. Then when they wanted to get more students to come to Marshall, I suggested that they put a large neon sign on Fifth Avenue in Huntington with hundreds of flashing lights on an arrow pointing toward the school reading: "GET YOUR COLLEGE DEGREE HERE. Drawing Saturday Night for a Free Master's Degree." The department chairperson moved my office into the basement of the library, a place no one ever went.

I noticed when I talked with country folks they were more willing to be candid if I wore blue jeans, chewed Mail Pouch, drove a truck, and didn't take notes. Folks who had known me and my family back on Williams Creek treated me with a slight degree of trepidation. Even old Oyer Clary, an old friend who used to drive past our house in a horse and buggy in the 1940s. My education and degrees were becoming a handicap. If I were ever to have to return to the working class, I would have to change my identity and start all over again. There was no way I was going back anyway unless I became a felon, but the thought was there. I had published a few personal essays about life in southern Ohio before I came to Marshall, most of them sentimental and biased toward how happy we were. Like those images we got about slaves that they lived and worked in the warm sun and sang so sad when massa went into the cold, cold ground. So I started digging around in my past, talking to folks back home, collecting data about good stories that had been handed down from generation to generation through talking. I also got some books and essays on Appalachian culture and history and studied up on the subject. First thing

Jo Ann Null collection

*Appalachian women, unidentified, circa 1930.*

to catch my attention was when I read stuff scholars were saying about the character, habits, and culture of Appalachia and the South, they were talking about my

*The author with five-year-old Elizabeth Farley, the family dog, and Elmer Farley.*

culture. But I was from Ohio, the buckeye state, a northern state if I ever heard of one. Not so. One-third of Ohio lies in Appalachia as defined by the Regional Commission. Part of that area is political to get federal money, but when you come down from Columbus and see the hills begin below Chillicothe you are in Appalachia for real. Gallia County borders on the Ohio River across from West Virginia, the only state lying entirely in Appalachia. The folks the scholars described sounded just like my family. I found out I was an Appalachian my own self. I began to write the stories I liked and, with a lot of luck, began to sell a few. Others I gave away. Writing is one of those arts that people will give away and even pay publishers to print their stories. That's your competition. But I remembered Will Durant, and here I paraphrase rather than parachute, "It's better to write one essay than read a thousand." To my surprise, even the local people I was writing about liked them. Well, they said they did. But I noticed folks wanted to make copies from the original rather than buy one. When an editor asked me to take a sentence out of a story and I was vexed, he said I want you to write for West Virginians, not about them. Another editor said always use crisp nouns and verbs; forget the adjectives and adverbs. The editors at the Ohio Historical Society told me to speak with an authoritative voice. Several editors just returned my work without comment. Bluegrass and gospel music had been a big influence on me. The more I wrote and tried to develop a style, I listened to the old-fashioned music of Bill Monroe, Ralph Stanley, Del McCoury, and the young gal from Champaign, Illinois, Alison Krauss. They sang and played the songs and tones of my youth, sounds I had once run from toward Frank Sinatra. I like the simple words, the mournful riffs, and the sad tones in the voices and instruments. Bluegrass and my experience tells me that Appalachians are folks who know how to get by. We press on in the struggle, most likely showing little or no self-pity. This collection contains most of my essays except for the 60 or so professional publications. I don't recommend anyone read those. This book is the Fulks canon. Or at least a Saturday night special. My philosophy of life, like most of my friends from the hills, is summed up in this bit Alison Krauss said while the band tuned during a concert: "Scratch it if it itches/Even if it's in your britches." And me, I'm still trying to figure out what a muse is.

# About the Author

Danny Fulks grew up on a farm in southern Ohio where his parents worked the land and milked cows. The old timers on Williams Creek say he never struck a lick of work in his life. He did, however, change spark plugs a few times on the propeller engines that pulled Boeing KC-97s during the Korean War. Fulks taught school in Gallia County, Ohio, was a school principal there and also in Franklin County. He has a doctor's degree from the University of Tennessee, is Professor Emeritus, Marshall University in West Virginia, and currently serves as an adjunct professor at Ohio University, Ironton branch. He has published a right smart including stories for *The MacGuffin*, *Goldenseal*, *Timeline*, *Now and Then*, *Hearthstone*, and *In Buckeye Country*, a collection published by Bottom Dog Press, Huron, Ohio. His collection, *Tales Along The Appalachian Plateau* came out in 1995. Recent stories include "First String" for *Appalachian Love Stories* published by the Jesse Stuart Foundation, "Clyde Raymond Beatty, Bainbridge, Ohio's Cat Man" for *Timeline*, and the section on Bevo Francis for the *Encyclopedia of Appalachia* for East Tennessee State University. He has been interviewed about his writing for ESPN and WOSU Television. Ohio, Kentucky, and West Virginia provide the setting for most of his stories covering such topics as food, murder, humor, sports, religion, Mail Pouch barns and barn lore, music, moonshine, cave exploration, life on the Ohio River, how to chew tobacco, and pretty much anything an editor will pay for. Danny Fulks's work is an important source for those who wish to know how much southeastern Ohio is like greater Appalachia and the south. Literary critics from the eastern establishment will say this is Fulks's oeuvre with a little bit of his metier thrown in for good measure. And hey, what about his muse? When this happens, Fulks will demand a retraction.

The author lives in Huntington, West Virginia.

e-mail: fulks@marshall.edu

# Special Thanks

Thanks to Pam Hill, Christopher Duckworth, Eddy Pendarvis, Jane Woodside, Ken Sullivan, Jim Gifford, Eric Cunningham, Gordon Simmons, Phyllis Moore, Margot Durbin, Larry Smith, Lenny Deutsch, Vin Cannameia.

And...Lance Thompson, Bertie Roush, Wayne White, Doris Gettys, Linda Wallace, Lester Stevers, Dale Holschuh, Carl Johnson, Bill Hayes, Duane Null, Brandy Rankin, Janice Stanley, Mariam Doughman, Blanch Spears, Buddy Kaiser, Susan Capper, Henrietta Evans, Estivaun Matthews, Mary Lee Marchi, Melissa Bentley, Susan Stinnett, Kara Loving, Jessica Jezerski, Tracy Hoskins, June Gregg, Atlee Fulks, Georgia Fulks, Buddy Kaiser, John Drinko, Gwen Dempsey, James Casto, Martha Woodward, Marci Atkins, Katie Mullins, Ruth Drummond, Jason Gorgia, George Lies, Gweneth Wickline, Amy Thompson, Dave Peyton, Jean Cooper, Clyde Evans, Newt Oliver, Vicki Wilson, Larry Varney, Lois Eanes, Jo Ann Null, Paula Newsome, Gerald Sutphin, Barbara Scott, Katie Captain, Lois Meadows, Virginia Bryant, Megan Benton, Bret Nance.

Special thanks to Alison Krauss and Union Station (Dan Tyminski, Ron Block, Barry Bales, and Jerry Douglas) who have brought the music of the author's youth into the 21st century with splendid riffs, tones, licks, arpeggios, humor, irony, and love, wrapped around Alison's alluring voice.